Reforming
Christianity

Reforming Christianity

DON CUPITT

Polebridge Press

Reforming Christianity

Library of Congress Cataloging-in-Publication Data

Cupitt, Don
  Reforming Christianity / Don Cupitt.
     p. cm.
  Includes bibliographical references and index.
  ISBN 0-944344-82-8 (pbk : alk. paper)
    1. Christianity. 2. Secularization (Theology) I. Title

BT83.7 .C87 2001
230--dc21

2001016339

For
Brian Hebblethwaite

Contents

Foreword

Although it is not necessary, it helps to read *Reforming Christianity* at 27,000 feet. My first acquaintance with Don Cupitt's latest work came on a thunderstorm-troubled flight from Dayton to Atlanta. As I looked up from the manuscript, I noticed that we had flown above the clouds to escape the weather. Ancient eyes would expect heaven to be outside the window. But from this modern chariot of the gods, where dreams are cast in aluminum and powered by jet fuel, there was no heaven, just a brilliant blue curving over the world.

Don Cupitt's critics have accused him often of reducing the multi-course banquet of the Christian tradition to a meager in-flight meal. They have become irritated at a man who prefers plain speech to propaganda. Instead of playing the ecclesiastical apologist, Cupitt decided long ago to be outrageous by not writing an untruthful book. He does not cover up but tells it like it is.

Cupitt's honesty comes from what can be called an "aerial view." He has followed the implications of the contemporary cultural discussion to gain a lucid perspective. Just as the view from the sky re-orients long familiar landscapes, rising beyond the confines of our tribal skylines, so Cupitt offers us a challenge to reimagine the very way we see our life on the face of the planet.

Unlike many philosophers of religion, Cupitt has not constructed a firewall against the critical thinkers of the modern world. As a conscious heir of the Enlightenment, he explores Kant's insight that we fabricate our world. Hegel has taught him that reality emerges in our encounter with historical developments. The confluence of physics, biology, and psychology makes an indelible mark on his writing. Cupitt has been labeled an apostate and a reductionist for his attempts to follow the critical paths blazed by Schopenhauer and Freud, Nietzsche and Wittgenstein, Heidegger and Derrida. Actually, we can say that Cupitt is drafting what Dietrich Bonhoeffer only intimated in his final correspondence: the profile of a religionless Christianity.

Not only the intellectuals have declared that the traditional philosophical underpinnings have broken down, we ourselves in our daily living intuitively recognize the inadequacy of maintaining belief in another world. Even a conservative believer today will see nothing more from an airplane window than the sky. Only an elaborate and overworked imaginative apparatus will buttress the conviction that there is an invisible world beyond the blue.

Cupitt asks us if we want to grow up. Do we need any longer to be lied to? Do we want to join the global shift away from authoritarianism and traditionalism? Can we see beyond the crippling assumption that the world is ready-made and that our human task is simply to be enthralled? Shall we finally enter the land of the free?

Or would we rather join with the churches now circling the wagons against the blasphemy of post-modernity? We could give up the world altogether hoping to catch a dubious murmur behind an outlandish screen. We could try to keep up, not just appearances, but the belief that there is something behind it all. Yet we know what Dorothy discovered in Oz. The demanding, sovereign Other was never there. Underneath that heated barking stood only humans in need.

Not just the eternal realm has collapsed as its supporting myths fall to earth like aging satellites. The nineteenth-century locomotive of pre-ordained progress also has been derailed. A century of war, genocide, atomic blackmail, and economic rampage has ushered in a democratic refusal to believe unwittingly in the inevitable. We have come to see the mythic narratives determining the actions of historical players. We have begun to understand that these foundational stories do not lead into the beyond whether in space or in time. Rather, they bring us back to earth, to the human beings responsible for their telling and the social worlds constructed from them.

What then is left? The only world there is. Cupitt contends that it is time for us to live with a clear-eyed recognition of life's finitude and transience. In his disarming style Cupitt turns our imaginations around. Although historical perspective takes much away, it delivers new vistas. By attending to the features most people would avoid by clinging to a timeless realm, Cupitt investigates the rank contingency of things. He does not deviate from the realization that there is no outside, that this is all we have and it is ours to make.

To catch Cupitt's creative move, an illustration may help. Consider the simple brilliance of a Möbius strip. Imagine cutting out a rectangular strip of paper. Number one side of the strip "1" and write "2" on the other side. Then, before joining the two ends to make a circle, twist one end 180° before taping the ends together. Now run your fingers along the path of one side throughout an entire circuit. Try it again. What you find out is that you

have formed a one-sided surface by that simple twist. This graphically illustrates the startling contention of Cupitt. The stories we spin do not lead to some other world. There is no other side. Life through a conscious twist becomes a sacred continuum. Evolution takes a critical turn through and by us. In the very midst of contingency, finitude and transience our life becomes endless, outsideless, as we give ourselves to life's immanent interconnection.

Precisely because of his contingent perspective Cupitt can re-envision the Christian traditions. The church becomes exposed for what it has been doing almost from the outset. It began by making excuses for Jesus' continued absence; it continues by justifying its own operation and muffling the words of the historical Jesus. Unable to entirely forget Jesus' nagging vision of the Kingdom, the church has deferred it for the time being. While the church has suspended Jesus in the heavens, the dysfunctional control of the church has kept Christians on their knees. But the world did not stand still while the church held its breath. Modernity blew off the ecclesiastical roof and left "bare ruined choirs" under an open sky. Main line churches are on the verge of becoming tourist traps, while the Holy leaks out, diffused throughout our human habitat.

In the midst of this collapse and uproar Cupitt tries to make out "the scratchy echo" of the historical Jesus. Alert to the contemporary Jesus discussion, Cupitt has rightly distinguished the historical voice of Jesus from the later debates that put words into his mouth. He sees that the vision of the Kingdom still has life in it. He argues that Kingdom theology is the "truth of our times." He wonders along with us what the world would be like if we learn to relate ourselves to others and to life in Jesus' new way. What happens if that visionary, unstable peasant gets a chance not just to speak but to make sense in our world? For Cupitt it is time for Jesus to return. Are we willing to take one another, including that artisan, so seriously that we finally become real to each other?

Cupitt courageously stays on the point. He does not have the time to mystify, to cover up for the sake of self-interest. He does not have the time, because none of us have the time to waste it dishonestly. Here and now is the time and place to come alive. We should not be misled into deferring our lives for some big pension plan in the sky. He challenges us to discover whether the treasure of the Kingdom is right in front of us, not permanently postponed.

There is a further ironic twist to Cupitt's argument. While it is too late to restore the church and the credibility of its doctrine (due to its internal power games and self-interest) it is still possible to see that genuine reformation has been long underway. The manifold secular experiments from the Enlightenment on indicate that the kingdom theology has already entered the cultural bloodstream. But religion itself can be seen from a creative angle. Just as modern drama had its roots in the medieval church so now religious congregations can become the launching pads for the communities' dreams, for detecting how our life and our world can be made better.

Such a dynamic revision should be congenial to an American audience. For the reader will soon come to note that Cupitt's book is a jazz performance. He thinks in riffs. His chapters are short interpretations of all there is, elaborations in different keys. He writes not to render us silent but to get us up on our feet and into the swing of things, to have us join in on what there really is, to jam along, and to lose ourselves, soaring gloriously, for as long as the music lasts.

Arthur J. Dewey
Xavier University
Christmas 2000

Introduction

The Christian churches are melting away: in Europe, at least, on most of the indices of measurable decline they are currently losing almost a quarter of what's left in each decade, and a half in each generation. The main reason for their decline is a general loss of public confidence in the objective truth of the major Christian beliefs. Until the late nineteenth century, church leaders honestly believed that a good and plausible rational case could be made in public for the truth of Christian doctrines; but today they know it can't, and nobody is even trying to develop a full-scale Christian metaphysics any more.[1]

What has happened? In the first place, the traditional philosophical underpinnings of faith – the arguments for the existence and attributes of God, and for the existence, the moral freedom and the immortality of the human soul – have all broken down. The old Christian natural philosophy has been replaced by the world view of natural science, and the basic assumptions of traditional religion, such as the division of the world of human experience into the two great realms of the sacred and the profane, have disappeared. Because society is no longer tradition-directed in the old way, we no longer assume that our life must always be framed by a fixed body of revealed truth that is taught by the Church and in the Bible. In the Muslim world, public debate still takes place within a general acceptance of the perpetuity of Islam as providing society's basic framework. To that extent, Islam as a great territorial and cultural fact still exists – but 'Christendom' does not. Over the past century or two, biblical criticism has eroded away the old generally acknowledged authority of the Bible as a public standard of religious truth. We no longer hear One Voice in the Bible: we hear only a crowd of different human voices.

In response to their growing difficulties, most forms of Christianity have since the late nineteenth century progressively lowered their sights, retreating into traditionalism, authoritarianism, and a view of 'faith' as effectively licensing anyone to believe anything. The result is that Christian preaching and writing have lost general intelligibility, and have come to sound more and more like the internal jargon of a cult. The Churches, inevitably, have steadily lost respect and self-respect.

No church has been more disastrously affected by these developments than my own church, the Church of England. As recently as 1845,

1

2 Reforming Christianity

John Henry Newman could seriously think that in leaving the Church of England to become a Roman Catholic he was leaving a great church for a lesser one. The standing of the English Church, both social and intellectual, still seemed to be unsurpassed in Christendom. The contrast with today's situation scarcely needs to be described. Yet nobody is talking about reform: on the contrary, provided that the necessary doctrinally conservative noises are made, any sort of irrationality is readily tolerated, whilst the hapless revisionist who attempts to put forward a rationally defensible modern interpretation of Christianity finds himself instantly in a state of permanent social exclusion.

It may be thought that the very idea of religious reform in the modern West is out-of-date. In the Arab world, Islamic doctrine still supplies the basis for a publicly authoritative Order of Reason to which all are subject. But in the modern democratic West we no longer have a great overarching public Order of Reason in the old, strong metaphysical and religious sense (unless it can be said that in the United States of America the Constitution occupies something close to that position). In general, in the modern West, what remains authoritative whoever is in power is merely technological and bureaucratic rationality (i.e., belief in *efficiency*). We are fluid and pluralistic; we are no longer Rationalists in the old, strong, capital R way. We no longer believe in a great body of Truth out there, waiting to be heard.

In that case, why am I talking about a rationalizing reformation of Christianity? In reply, I am not suggesting that Christianity can or should be restored to the kind of public standing that it once had in Europe, and that Islam still has in the Arab world. On the contrary, my reformed Christianity will be *post-dogmatic*, in the sense that it will not pretend to be putting forward any publicly authoritative supertruths. It will simply aim to show how the profession and practice of a thoroughly reformed version of Christianity could again come to look attractive to a thinking person, *after* dogma, and *after* the Church. In a pluralist democratic society people are rightly suspicious of ideologies that make totalizing claims, and we should be content to propose Christianity as offering a form of life that is true − not absolutely, because we are giving up that idea − but which *rings true to* our sense of ourselves, *true to* the way things currently are, and *true to* our life as we now live it.

In passing, it is worth repeating that in giving up dogma we are giving up the idea of revealed truth and acknowledging that all versions of Christianity, from the oldest to the newest, are simply what the historian knows them to be, namely human cultural formations. 'Orthodoxy' is a myth invented by the powerful by way of consolidating and extending their power. In fact, there never was an original pure essence of Christianity (. . . that became corrupted over the centuries, and now needs to be recovered, etc).[2] So I do not and cannot claim that my reformed Christianity represents a return to something purer, more authentic and more original. The past can never really be recovered, and it is better to admit that we do not have access to any objective norm in these matters, and instead must judge religion as we judge art, by purely immanent and humanly established criteria. Along these lines we can continue to make a clear distinction between good and bad religion, even though we have no universal and readymade criteria of religious truth. Thus I can say that our current church Christianity makes far too many grand claims that it can no longer justify, that it is manifestly in steep decline, and that it no longer works well *just as religion*, and is not imaginatively productive. It is not producing any architecture or art or texts or lives that really *matter*. It makes no difference. Until as recently as the 1960s church Christianity was still making a worthwhile contribution to our developing humanitarian ethics, and so long as worthwhile moral initiatives were still coming from the churches it was worth staying with them; but now even that has stopped, and the recent slide of the churches into phobic moralism has been the last straw. In effect, church Christianity is over. It is not going to reform itself: it couldn't do so, even if it wanted to. It no longer has enough energy and strength of will to change itself. So those of us who care about the continuation of the Christian tradition will do best to stop worrying about the Church and try to develop a new form of religious life that will be genuinely truthful, liveable and productive. Whether or not it wishes to brand itself Christian does not in the end matter very much. I can well understand the point of view of those who say that the brand name 'Christian' has become so badly tarnished by many of those who currently trade under it, that they for their part would prefer not to use it.

However, I still have a personal feeling for the old brand name. One of the stimuli for attempting a new reformation today is the well-known fact that historic orthodox Christianity was based upon an almost outrageously bad misinterpretation of the meaning and the message of the original Jesus. But for all sorts of reasons, the kingdom religion of the original Jewish teacher is nowadays more interesting (and even, more up-to-date) than the elaborate machinery of sacramentally mediated, promised and yet deferred salvation that grew up around the God Incarnate of church religion. Jesus, with his very exceptional combination of end of the world urgency, humanitarianism and even a form of nihilism, now looks much more interesting than the traditional Christian misreading of him. So I want to cling on for a while yet to the old brand name, and to the Jewish teacher who somehow began it all. It is time he was given a chance to speak; time for him to return, at last.

A second reason why church Christianity is dying is that it is not putting forward any sort of credible and attractive picture of the religious life. It is too thin, *as religion*. After 'going to church', believing the right doctrines, 'saying your prayers', and paying up, what is there? Until the 1960s Christian ethics was still much respected, and Christians were active in the founding and the development of major new humanitarian charities. Today, the public reputation of Christian ethics has crashed, amidst far too much evidence of great unhappiness and truly malignant human relations within the churches. There has been too much child abuse, rampant misogyny and homophobia, and reflex fear and hostility towards new technical and scientific developments, especially in medicine and in genetics. In some places there has been too much collusion with nationalism. It is not surprising that public bodies are no longer quite so keen to have church representatives on ethics committees.

It is very characteristic of our period that a writer like Iris Murdoch should have had much of interest to say about the religious life, without herself being a practising Christian. The churches and religion have become disconnected from each other. And it is against such a background that I am suggesting that although it may now be too late to restore the Church and the credibility of Christian doctrine, we may nevertheless be able to do something in the way of putting forward an intelligible and attractive account of a Christian form of the religious life.

Chapter One

Reforming Christianity

With a few small exceptions, such as the first generation and the Society of Friends, church christianity is just about the only kind of Christianity that most people have known hitherto. Today it is in rapid decline: but there is little public discussion of Christianity's non-ecclesiastical forms, and little discussion of the possibility of a reformation and renewal of the old faith, even at this late hour. The very suggestion that this time what needs to be reformed is not just the Church, but *the Faith itself*, can of course be relied upon to disturb all those people whose thinking about religion remains traditional rather than critical. But everyone who has studied Christian origins and the subsequent history of the Early Church is nowadays familiar with the suggestion that there was nothing necessary about the way Christianity happened to develop. The earliest Christianity was an untidy jumble of different schools of thought. Eventually a dominant faith emerged, which claimed to be orthodox and legitimate, and called other views heretical. It even claimed to be original; but the New Testament itself shows that there was no single original and authentic faith. The development might have followed a different path, and perhaps it should have done. Furthermore, there has already been one previous Reformation, at the end of the Middle Ages; so why should we not consider the possibility of another, now that we find ourselves plunged into an even more profound cultural upheaval? In the 1960s the possibility of a New Reformation was at least discussible; so why should not the idea return today?

Some people are certainly going to resist the suggestion that what they call 'the Gospel', and insist is 'the same yesterday, and today, and forever', is a human construct, wildly at odds with the original Jesus and his message, that now doesn't work any more and needs to be replaced with something better and truer that *does* work properly. But I am going to try to change their minds. Briefly (and as I have already indicated elsewhere) the cultural changes we are going through are so great that they demand a major revolution in religious thought. The deep assumptions that underlay traditional religious and philosophical thinking have long ago broken down, and must be given up. In the new situation, I shall argue, the best response is to push Christianity on into the next (and final) stage of its historical development.[1] This means, in traditional theological language, moving religious thought on from 'ecclesiastical theology' to 'kingdom theology', because it was classically believed that the age of the Church would eventually be followed by the return of Jesus and a new Messianic Age, variously called the Millennium, the New Jerusalem, or the Kingdom of Christ. This meant and means a move from the *mediated* kind of religion with which we are familiar, to the *immediate* kind of religion that people have always believed possible and have hoped for, if not in this life, then at least after death.

The man whose teaching sparked off the development of Christianity, Jesus of Nazareth, preached the here and now possibility of immediate religion. He called it by a curious and rather new name, 'the Kingdom of God', and he prophesied the destruction of the chief symbol of mediated religion in his own milieu, namely 'the Temple'. But he died without seeing the Kingdom become clearly established, and after his death the Kingdom still seemed to be delayed. The Church and its teaching then gradually developed as a stopgap, an interim organization filling in the awkward intercalary period between the promise of the Kingdom and its awaited fulfilment. The Church's job was to gather and prepare an organized body of vigilant believers who would be awake and ready for the Kingdom when at last it came.

The subsequent history of the Church can be divided into three or four stages. In the first stage, the Church's teaching consists of a string of reasons for the awkward delay in the full manifestation of the Kingdom. In current Jewish belief a general resurrection of the dead was to take place at the end of all things. Now Jesus was believed to be raised, and some claimed that others too had already risen with him (e.g. Matt 27:51–3). Therefore the Kingdom really was beginning. But there was a difficulty: the risen Lord was visible only to believers, only to the eye of faith. Otherwise, the world seemed to be going on just as before. Why was Jesus absent, and why the delay? The Church replied that Jesus seemed to be absent because he was for the present offstage. God had exalted Jesus to a seat at his own right hand; but his absence in Heaven was only temporary. He would soon return to earth in glory as Messiah and Judge (e.g. Acts 1:11, 3:17–21).

Thus the primitive church began to look up to and to worship an ascended Lord and Christ, calling upon him to come back soon: and it is to be noted that at this primitive stage faith in a Christian dogma takes the form of belief that something presently hidden in the invisible world will shortly be made manifest in this world. Such was the earliest form that dogma took: it was an expression of eschatological hope.

Then, at stage two in the sub-apostolic period, the Church begins to develop as a complex system of mediated religion. It has got the beginnings of a system of *beliefs*; it has the beginnings of the *sacraments*, through which people are ritually marked out as belonging to Christ and as waiting for his coming, and it has in the Apostles and their associates the beginnings of an officer class, the Hierarchy, who are the rulers of the Church. In time they came to control all aspects of the Church's life, and even to think of themselves as *being* 'the Church': a Council of all the Bishops is an Ecumenical Council of *the Church*.

Then, at stage three, fully worked out ecclesiastical Christianity – 'Catholicism' – begins to develop during the later second century, or thereabouts. The Kingdom is now deferred so far into the future that it effectively vanishes over the horizon of history. The Church is no longer a temporary holding operation but a permanent fact. Until the end of time it is indefectible, and it even came eventually to think of itself as being infallible. Doctrinal beliefs, which had begun as excuses for the temporary absence of Jesus and his new Kingdom world, are now your personal passport to Heaven. You are not preparing for him to come to you: you are preparing yourself to go to him. Life is to be spent in readying oneself for death. In the church, sacramental Grace is administered according to strict rules by a highly bureaucratic salvation machine that processes souls en masse for Heaven. Everyone's first concern in life must be for her own eternal salvation, to which the Church holds the only key. This world is unimportant except as a proving ground. Ethics for the ordinary person is highly individualistic; it has become chiefly a matter of avoiding occasions of sin and trying to ensure that one dies in a state of grace.

At stage four, in the later Middle Ages, a few people begin to say in one way or another that mediated religion has become a monstrous idol, the grandest and most 'total' institution that human beings have ever created. The system of mediated religion, the great salvation machine, no longer points beyond itself: on the contrary, it makes sure that we understand that its jurisdiction will never come to an end. Its doctrines, once temporary reasons for absence and promises of a speedy return, are now metaphysical dogmas certified by an infallible teacher. The system of mediation, the set of proper channels, has now become in effect *itself* the religious object. Whether the whole system actually points to a real transcendent Object beyond it no longer matters much, because *we never find out*. The believer believes in the Pope, the Creed, the Church and the Sacraments: intellectual and moral thraldom to the machine is what gives to ordinary believers the sense of security that they have come to think of as being 'faith' and as true religion. Even to this day, most people in effect define a Christian as a person who holds a particular set of doctrinal beliefs and is subject to a particular 'obedience'.

We need not here describe the ways in which the Church overreached itself and began to provoke dissent on the part of mystics, protestants, and rebellious theologians. Suffice it to say that during the later nineteenth century the Death of God forced the issue. Amongst other things, it has the effect of shifting the focus of attention permanently and decisively back to this world, the human world, the life world. The huge apparatus of otherworldly and mediated religion suddenly looks hollow and threadbare. What on earth was it for? Why did we put up with it for so long? Why did we allow it to poison our feeling for life by persuading us that our real happiness can begin only on the far side of death?

To raise these questions is of course to hint at the name of Nietzsche, and at the moment in the later nineteenth century when Western culture began to change direction. A whole series of deep philosophical and religious assumptions, by which people had almost always been guided hitherto, now began to break down. The end of metaphysics – the end of belief in a more real eternal world beyond the world of our present life – forces people to give up ulteriority, and to concentrate their whole attention on this present life of ours in all its contingency and its temporality. A good deal of philosophy and religious thought turns in the direction of what would come to be called Existentialism. The old commitment to *God* is increasingly translated into commitment, first to 'existence', and then to 'life'.

Against this background I am suggesting that today the reformation of Christianity must proceed by going back to the beginning in order to go forwards. It is necessary to recall the curiously complicated story of the Faith's first origins and early development, in order to see why it is now time to abandon Church theology and push the Christian movement forwards into the next and long promised stage of its historical development: the Kingdom. The Kingdom is purely of this present world: it is a new ethic, and a new way of relating oneself to life. It is post-ecclesiastical and post-dogmatic. We've been praying daily for it all these years. Now, its time has come.

The Kingdom is pure religious immediacy. In Israel as in so many religious systems, there was a contrast between being ruled by God *through* a King who is his earthly representative, and being ruled by God directly. When God ruled his people directly — as in the ideal past, and again in the ideal future — it was by coming to dwell amongst them and by putting his own Spirit in their hearts, so that they would obey the divine Law spontaneously and without inner conflict. Amazingly, self-expression and moral conduct just *coincide*. Thus immediate religion is no more than semi-realist about God: God is very close to the believer, indwells the believer, and is indeed almost concentric with the believer. And some such state is evidently what Jesus envisages when he talks about the Kingdom of God, and says that it is 'among' or 'within' (*entos*) you. The Kingdom 'grows secretly'; it 'comes upon' us. God is no longer an Other in apposition to the believer, but is fully internalized. Hence the very striking inwardness or hiddenness of God in the teaching of Jesus. God is so close that he disappears. The religious world simply coincides with the life world, and everything becomes holy.

An alternative way to make the point about the disappearance of the old objective God in kingdom religion is to follow the route taken by Albert Schweitzer, who was a student of Kant and a non-realist about God. Schweitzer held that we should be true to history and acknowledge that Jesus expected the kingdom to be brought in by a supernatural act of God. But nowadays we do not hold that world view, and instead see God in a non-realistic way as personifying the moral requirement. In which case it is up to *us* to bring in the kingdom by our ethical striving. Schweitzer's non-realism about God thus permitted him to be truthful *both* about the historical Jesus *and* about how things are for us today.

These ideas however are not congenial to church people, who are enthusiastic for theological realism and mediation. They project God out as a mysterious, demanding, sovereign Other, overwhelmingly out there and over against the believer. The infinite qualitative difference between God and the believer makes a happy religious relationship between them impossible, and a Mediator is needed to bridge the gap. In ecclesiastical Christianity the exalted Jesus becomes the Mediator, and the whole vast system of mediation — the Church, its ministers, the sacraments, the Scriptures and the creeds — all belong to him and testify to him. Against that background one can understand why it came to be an article of faith that the Son of God Incarnate, the Mediator, is co-equally and co-eter-nally God of God, and also fully human as we are. The idea was to guarantee the religious efficacy of the system of mediation; but by the same token the way was opened for the great system of mediation to become *itself* the supreme religious object. If God is objective, infinite and incomprehensible, and Jesus Christ the Mediator is the only way to God, then Jesus is in effect the only god for us; and if he is present to us in the form of the mighty apparatus of religious mediation, the Church of which he is the foundation and the guarantor, then a kind of idolatry of the Church is unavoidable. And so it turned out: Church Christianity eventually turned into the last great form of idolatry.[2] So at least the great Protestant Reformers thought (but they didn't fully overcome it, alas).

All this indicates why ecclesiastical Christianity as we have received it in the days of its decline is so oddly blurred and confused. In the Synoptic Gospels we can still hear a scratchy echo of the voice of the original Jesus, the Jewish prophet of the Kingdom of God who wants us simply to choose and to live religious immediacy right away. But the New Testament also contains documents which teach a very different theology, and which see Jesus as the nucleus around which a huge new system of religious mediation will be elaborated. The critic and opponent of religious mediation was thus made into the basis of a new religious system of just the kind he died opposing. Hence Nietzsche's saying that there has been only one Christian, and he died on a cross. That is roughly correct.

It has taken us a long time to grasp and to admit how profoundly ecclesiastical Christianity has misunderstood and misrepresented Jesus. Perhaps if the Gospel of John had not got into the New Testament canon we would even yet not have noticed the contradiction between the religion Jesus taught, and the religion of which he was later made the basis. Certainly in the nineteenth century, and in writers like D.F. Strauss, it was the wide gap between the Synoptic Gospels and St John's Gospel that first showed people just how far Christianity must have travelled during its early development. In the Synoptics, Jesus is a human teacher who may be the Messiah; but in John Jesus is an incarnate divine being who comes to earth to reveal his own glory — and to this day it is the Johannine Jesus who is worshipped by the church. But today, when we see that ecclesiastical Christianity is coming to an end, we can contemplate the possibility of going back to the much higher kind of religion that the original Jesus announced. For there are reasons for thinking that we may now *at last* be ready for immediate religion.

It is amusing to think of someone who was 2000 years ahead of his time. That is a long time to have to wait to be understood, a long time to have to wait for one's followers and companions to come along.

An Ugly Little Man

Chapter
Two

In 1975 I had an opportunity to examine the very well preserved skeleton of a man who was crucified in first-century Palestine. The nail marks were in the expected places, just above the wrist and neatly between the radius and ulna of each arm, and – much more crudely and destructively – sideways through the two ankles together. He was tiny. He seemed like a boy: but we know from other archaeological evidence that the Palestinian Jews of late antiquity were small people by our standards.

The skeleton had been found about a mile NW of the Old City of Jerusalem. Inevitably, the thought crossed my mind that these could be the bones of Jesus. I thought of the ancient pagan writer Celsus, who in a book against the Christians argued that you would expect any man who had a divine spirit in him to be of distinguished appearance in some way. Celsus means, I suppose, that a θεῖος ἀνήρ, a divine man, should be tall, noble and with regular features, whereas (he says) Jesus was not at all like that: 'his body was, as they say, little, ugly and undistinguished'.[1] The Christian scholar Origen, replying to Celsus, does not deny the charge, which had earlier been referred to by a number of Christian authors, including Clement of Alexandria and Tertullian (both writing c. C.E. 200).

All these writers may have been influenced by the description of the 'Suffering Servant' of God as ugly in Isaiah 53. But there is also the fact that in the Gospel of Luke Jesus himself is portrayed as referring to the gibe, 'Physician, heal thyself!' The obvious implication of it is that Jesus personally suffered from one or another of the afflictions that he healed in others, but Luke's Jesus doesn't take it like that. He paraphrases it as saying: 'What we have heard you did at Capernaum, do here also in your own country', and he replies that 'No prophet is acceptable in his own

11

country'.[2] Matthew, following Luke, also seems to acknowledge a well-known gibe against Jesus, choosing to give it a soteriological interpretation. Jesus' enemies mock him on the cross by saying: 'He saved others: he cannot save himself'.[3]

Thus Matthew and Luke both seem to feel that they must acknowledge a strong tradition that Jesus' appearance was unprepossessing, and both of them seek rather clumsily to explain it away. The tradition lingered nevertheless, and for the next century or two it was customary to speak of Jesus as appearing in two distinct forms. In the days of his flesh the Lord had indeed been of 'dishonourable' appearance, but in his risen form as seen by the eye of faith he was of noble and beautiful aspect. Hence the reported difficulty of recognizing the Risen Lord.[4] He had changed considerably.

However, as the Christian tradition developed, and especially as Christian art began to develop, the old tradition of the lowly appearance of the human Jesus was overlaid and forgotten. It became usual to project back the glorious Greek-god risen appearance of Jesus into his earthly life. As we can already see happening in the Gospel of John, this drastically affected the way Jesus' teaching was understood and the way people understood his human life, his person and his work. In short, Jesus' original teaching fell into misunderstanding and neglect, and his life was no longer thought of as a normal human life. Instead, Jesus now comes to be thought of as God Incarnate, and his life becomes a stately procession through a series of theological tableaux, revelatory moments − *stills* − in each of which something of his eternal Glory is manifested in the spatio-temporal world. He is on earth in order to manifest himself in this way. Each tableau is a moment like the recognition scene in a Greek tragedy. It is a suprahistorical moment of revelation: at that instant, and there alone, the Eternal shines through.

This transformation of Jesus' life into a chain of theological tableaux, set pieces or 'stations', is most clearly demonstrated by the history of Christian art, both Eastern and Western.[5] Here we find that the number of canonical tableaux is about 50 (with a little extra elaboration in the 14 'Stations of the Cross'). These great set pieces are concentrated around the events of Jesus' conception, birth, crucifixion, death, burial and resurrection, because these events had become central to the orthodox understanding of his person and his work. Certain of Jesus' miracles, as spectacular demonstrations of his divine power, also developed into theological set pieces, but the everydayness of his lived human life and his moral teaching never made it into the Creed and was not commemorated anywhere, either in the Calendar or in the dedications of churches. So it largely dropped out, having become irrelevant. Ordinary life is not wanted.

So far as I know, nobody has yet thought it worth listing all the tableaux in their canonical sequence, and under their standard designations. They are as follows – but note that 15–19 stand a little apart from the rest:

The Infancy
1. The Annunciation
2. The Visitation
3. The Nativity
4. The Adoration of the Shepherds
5. The Adoration of the Magi, *or* Kings
6. The Madonna and Child
7. The Circumcision of Christ
8. The Presentation of Christ in the Temple
9. The Flight into Egypt
10. The Massacre of the Innocents
11. The Madonna and Child with the Infant St John (and Saint Anne or Elizabeth)
12. Christ Among the Doctors

The Ministry
13. The Baptism of Christ
14. Christ in the Wilderness
15. The Wedding Feast at Cana
16. Christ Healing the Paralytic at the Pool of Bethesda
17. Christ in the House of Simon the Pharisee (with Mary Magdalene)
18. The Raising of Jairus' Daughter
19. The Raising of Lazarus
20. The Transfiguration of Christ

The Passion
21. Christ's Entry into Jerusalem
22. The Cleansing of the Temple
23. The Last Supper
24. The Betrayal of Christ (to the Chief Priests by Judas)
25. The Agony in the Garden
26. The Kiss of Judas (and the Arrest of Christ)
27. Christ Before the High Priest / Peter Denying Christ

28. Christ Before Pilate
29. *Ecce Homo*
30. Pilate Washing His Hands
31. The Flagellation of Christ at the Pillar
32. The Crown of Thorns
33. The Mocking of Christ
34. The Procession to Calvary / Christ Carrying His Cross
35. The Veronica
36. Christ Waiting to be Crucified / The Man of Sorrows
37. The Crucifixion with
    A. The Soldiers Dividing Christ's Garments
    B. The BVM and St John
    C. The Penitent Thief
    D. 'I Thirst'
    E. The Piercing of Christ's Side
38. The Deposition / The Descent from the Cross
39. *Pietà*
40. The Entombment
41. The Dead Christ

The Resurrection
42. The Resurrection (with the Empty Tomb and the Soldiers)
43. The Three Maries at the Sepulchre
44. *Noli Me Tangere*
45. The Supper at Emmaus
46. Doubting Thomas
47. The Ascension of Christ

Subjects not tied to a particular event, or Feast
48. Christ Seated in Majesty (enthroned on the Firmament)
49. The Good Shepherd
50. The Light of the World
51. Christ's Commission to Peter / Christ giving the Keys to Peter

Many comments are called for at once. To make this list more authoritative, we would need to be able to consult a complete and iconograph-
ically classified database of Christian art – which does not yet exist. Numbers 15–19 stand outside the canonical sequence of all the other items:
they are typical examples of individual scenes from Christ's public ministry, but such scenes are always relatively uncommon in Christian art,
and almost *none* has become a canonical set piece with an accepted title
and iconographic history of its own.[6] The popular scenes involving Mary

Magdalene (including 17 and 44) seem to provide an erotic subtext to the life of Jesus, just as the equally popular scenes involving Salome do for the life of the Baptist.

Some tableaux are so popular that they develop various secondary ones linked to them. This happens most of all with the Passion Narrative, but can also be seen in the way that The Adoration of the Magi comes to be preceded by The Journey of the Magi, and the Flight into Egypt similarly develops a very popular Rest on the Flight into Egypt.

Elaboration happens in another way. The Life of Christ has become conformed to the general pattern of the life of an Eastern holy man. It resembles the Life of the Buddha, the Life of Mahavira (as it may be seen, for example, in the stained-glass windows of the Jain temple at Leicester, England), and the life of Appolonius of Tyana. And so powerfully is the archetypal pattern exemplified in Christ that it spreads to others associated with him. Thus the Blessed Virgin Mary develops a whole cycle of set-piece tableaux, ending with her Dormition, Assumption and Coronation, that closely parallels the Christ cycle. And the same is true to a lesser degree of the Baptist, and also of St Peter.

Considerations of evidence, historicity and consistency have evidently counted for very little, as one soon discovers when one tries to write down nos. 7–10 in the correct order, or when writing out the Mary cycle alongside the Christ cycle. Faith was perfectly happy simply to invent new subjects in order to meet popular demand. Apart from a single iconoclastic convulsion in the East, and a later one at the Reformation in the West, Christian art has at all times been very popular, and indeed populist. Reflecting the wishes of its patrons, it has very closely tracked the evolution of the Church and its various observances, and the development both of theology and of popular devotion. In fact, the history of Christian art is an excellent image of the history of Christianity itself, and what it shows us beyond doubt is the extent to which the huge entity we call 'Christianity' has been unashamedly *created*, by the very people who saw themselves as being its adherents or followers. Official theology represents the entire religious system as a sacred plenum, 'Holy Tradition', divinely instituted, divinely guaranteed and divinely preserved from error. People intensely and passionately feel and affirm its sacred objectivity: and yet historical study shows it to be a huge collective work of folk art, both cultural tradition and communal fantasy. People have created the religion they felt they needed, and having done so have been convinced of its objective givenness. An Argument from Design has been involved: our religion is so perfectly adapted to our natures that it must in all its details have been specially designed for us by a wise and benevolent Creator.

Like all versions of the Argument from Design, this one is invalid. No external Designer need be postulated, for it is much simpler and more in accord with the empirical evidence to suppose that it was we ourselves who created our own religion and adapted it to our needs. And why should we not cheerfully admit the obvious, and practise our religion just as we play our other human games – in the honest recognition of its purely human past history and present character? Why not? The last bit of supernatural Christianity that is still practised spontaneously by the bulk of the population is the School Nativity Play. Everyone knows that even in Matthew and Luke it was already only pious folktale, but everyone loves it. It's hokum, it's only a folk custom; but why shouldn't we practise our religion on just that 'non-realistic' basis?

To see why a non-realist understanding and practice of traditional Christianity will not do, and to see why we are now talking about *reforming* Christianity, we need to consider further the ways in which Christian art does and does not portray Christ. We will see that Christian art reveals something very instructive about Christian piety, namely that Christianity so far has been quite unable to picture either Mary or Jesus as having lived ordinary human lives.

NOTE

In a tradition-directed society an artist was never free to depict a sacred subject in any way he pleased. He always had to depict a standard scene, and he always had to follow very detailed iconographical rules. In Christian culture the effect of this was that the art tradition became a 'fifth gospel', imprinting upon the public mind just one image of Jesus, namely that of the Divine Saviour of ecclesiastical faith. People just *know* that Jesus had a beard, rose bodily from his tomb, and so on. To this day it remains difficult to interest people in the claim that critical historical research has found a Jesus who was quite unlike the Jesus of Italian art. Thus in the 1970s Franco Zeffirelli's lengthy film *Jesus of Nazareth* (1976) came out visually as a walk through the fifty standard tableaux – and perhaps it *had* to take this form, because the film would not have been recognized as a film about Jesus unless it had conformed to the very detailed, tradition-guided expectations of its audience. Zeffirelli's film had to copy the film that was already in people's heads, or they would have been very *angry* with him. They would have called him a blasphemer. Hence my problem in this book: to recover Jesus we have to over-come the whole tradition of Christian art, and that is not at all an easy thing to do. Nobody has yet been able to do it.

Chapter Three
Holiness and Leakage

I have said that in Christian art the lives of Jesus and of Mary (and to a lesser extent also of John the Baptist) were presented as chains of carefully-defined and rather static tableaux. Each tableau became a popular sermon-topic, for it was a Moment in which the Eternal had manifested itself in time. The action was frozen at the moment of recognition, or at the instant when divine power begins to be exerted. The preacher explained all this by describing the circumstances, and interpreting the symbols involved. This Moment is not a moment *within* the moving time of human interaction, but rather a Moment when human interaction has been 'frozen', so that attention is concentrated instead upon the Eternal which is shining through. Thus the whole temporal movement of Jesus' life with other people has been eliminated, and replaced by 50 freeze-frames. Ignatius Loyola is enough of a humanist to be a partial exception, for he encourages the meditator to think of Jesus' human life. But otherwise, for the main tradition, no revelation of the divine takes place, or *can* take place, in the temporal to-and-fro of ordinary human life; it can take place only in the fifty freezes. The eternal Son of God takes flesh and lives a human life *only in order that* his divinity can be symbolically revealed in the freezes. This is an oddly-reduced conception of the Incarnation. *Why?*

It is further to be noted that in Christian art the central figure, Jesus or Mary, is almost always a little withdrawn, separate, sad, passive, and reproachful-looking – usually with mouth firmly closed. Mary in particular is always heavily-swathed in clothing, like a nun, and her eyes are demurely downcast, as if she is the passive, willing victim of her own unique vocation. Nowhere in Christian art does she catch her husband's eye, or even glance at him. She is so holy that according to Catholic

19

belief her marriage was never consummated: her other children are denied, despite their frequent mention in the New Testament, and even giving birth to Jesus did not rupture her virginity. The strangeness of Christian art's treatment of Mary is brought out by those post-Christian works that set out to provoke the public by showing Mary in previously-unthinkable ways: thus, a well-known Spanish painting shows her spanking the infant Jesus for being naughty.

Jesus, similarly, in Christian art very commonly wears a somewhat distant and reproachful expression. The Synoptic Gospels portray him as having positively *relished* the cut-and-thrust of argument with various groups of his critics and enemies, yet I think nowhere in Christian art is Jesus depicted engaged in animated conversation. A taciturn Jew is a prodigy indeed. And Jesus' shrinking back from others extends also to his physical behaviour, most eloquently in various treatments of the *Noli me tangere* subject. A holy person cannot risk being compromised. He must remain a little apart. Any sort of *intercourse*, sexual or behavioural or even merely conversational, threatens to cause his holiness to leak away, as is well brought out by the case of the polluted woman with a haemorrhage who touched the hem of his garment (Luke 8:46, compare Luke 7:39). Contact with a woman was regarded as being potentially defiling and weakening, especially for soldiers and (in our own society) seamen, miners and some sportsmen.

Holiness means separation: that is the basic reason why the Christian imagination was never able to picture either the Incarnate Lord or his Mother as having lived fully human lives. St Benedict saw clearly that a Christian monk must live apart from ordinary people, and *a fortiori* the Holiest Ones of all must have done so.

The story needs to be told: in Leviticus, in Ezekiel 40–48, and elsewhere in the Hebrew Bible we find all the classic religious ideas about holiness worked out in great detail. The double distinction, between the holy and the common and between the clean and the unclean, is a fundamental principle of religion and neatly illustrates the way religion structures our world and gives us our basic cosmology. Clear distinctions must be made and respected all over the world of our experience, between what is clean and what is unclean and between the holy and the common. The principal holy thing, whose integrity we must try to preserve, is the human body. Great care has to be taken about anything that crosses the boundary between the body and the external world. One must eat only clean foods, and purify oneself after any polluting discharges from the body. In women, menstruation and childbirth create a state of uncleanness (e.g. Leviticus 12), skin diseases such as leprosy create a very serious state of uncleanness, and in a number of societies wounds and injuries make men unclean.

These classical ideas about holiness are very familiar, and for modern readers have been particularly clearly explained by the anthropologist Mary Douglas.[1] They still do play some part in the Gospel narratives. But there is also a suggestion both in the teaching of Jesus and in the Acts of the Apostles that in the new world traditional ideas about the line between the clean and the unclean are to be violently shaken up, or even simply abolished (e.g. Mark 7:14–23; Acts 10:1–11:18). In the Gentile Church everything will be 'cleansed': everyone will be holy and nothing will be unclean.

It did not last: as 'Christianity' developed into a very large system of mediated religion almost all the old ideas about the holy and the common, the clean and the unclean, came back. The effect was in the end to make it unimaginable that a perfectly holy person could live an entirely normal human life in the world, either as a woman or as a man; the difficulty being that time and change and every sort of intercourse with others always threaten to cause a leakage of holiness and a loss of 'power'. Neither Jesus nor Mary can possibly risk being fully committed to ordinary life: and in art we notice that neither of them is ever really *at ease*.

People often make the mistake of supposing that Christians are especially anxious about sex. That is an oversimplification. Because sex involves mingling of bodies and body fluids, it is especially likely to cause loss of bodily integrity and leaking-away of holiness; but the same is also true of every other sort of 'mingling' with other people in the world. The point is very clearly made by the idioms that we still use when we exhort a shy person who is nervously hanging back to join in some communal activity. *Muck in!,* we say in England, meaning that he must overcome his fear of defilement. *Get stuck in!,* we say, with vivid sexual overtones: *Mingle!,* don't be afraid of commitment: *Get involved! Lend a hand!:* contribute your own body's output to the common task. *Don't be afraid to get your hands dirty.* These idioms show that religious anxiety about sex is only one instance of a much more general anxiety about one's physical cleanness, integrity or holiness. *Any* kind of mingling or intercourse with others is felt to threaten defilement and a draining-away of one's power. Especially for men who face some kind of ordeal or battle or special danger, it is thought best to conserve one's strength by sticking to the company of one's own sex and avoiding women.

Christian apologists often argue that the Incarnation of God in Christ has made everything holy. But on the contrary, the belief that God had become incarnate in Jesus evolved as part of the process by which

'Christianity' developed into a new and very elaborate form of mediated religion, which reinstated all the old ideas about the sacred and the profane, the clean and the unclean, and prolonged their life until only a very few years ago. Even today there are many people for whom 'the religious life' has to be a celibate life.

The effect of this has been to introduce a weird contradiction into mainstream Christianity, both Greek and Latin. On the one hand the Church insisted that Jesus the Son of God Incarnate and his Holy Mother had both been real people who had lived fully human lives; but on the other hand the archaic ideas about the holy and the unclean to which the Church was (and still is) committed made it impossible to imagine how either Jesus or Mary could have lived a human life in time. Holiness requires separation and self-distancing from others, to preserve one's innocence and integrity. But human social life in time is always a continuous living process of *exchange*, physical, sexual, economic and semiotic. We are *mingling*, taking in bits of others and giving away bits of ourselves. We simply do not and cannot *both* live an ordinary human life *and* preserve our own identity and integrity undefiled. So when we read the New Testament we still find ourselves assuming that Jesus, Mary, the Baptist, the Twelve Apostles, Paul, Timothy, Barnabas and the rest must all of them be living celibate lives, despite indications in the text to the contrary.

All of this is by way of an explanation of the fact that Christian art, trying to imagine the human life of God Incarnate, could not come up with anything better than a chain of some fifty or so static tableaux, which preachers interpret as moments when the Eternal has manifested itself symbolically in the temporal world. And when trying to imagine the human being who was the Mother of God, the Christian imagination could not do better than picture her as a woman who was scarcely a woman at all. The Church's message was fatally subverted by its own ideas about the holy, ideas that seem to be older, deeper and stronger than the Church's surface doctrines about God and Christ.

We now see the meaning of the famous remark that when in the nineteenth century Ernest Renan and others began to write novels about the life of Jesus, orthodox Christianity was at an end. For if you make Jesus into a character in a novel, you must picture him as a genuine human being living in time and in processes of exchange; and you must therefore have dispensed with both the doctrine of the Incarnation and the ideas about holiness and uncleanness that have been fundamental to nearly all of traditional religion hitherto.

Two supplementary points now need to be made. First, exactly the same difficulty occurs in the tradition of Western philosophy that stems from Plato and Aristotle. People have wished to keep and to privilege rather strong ideas of substance and of identity. Substance is philosophy's version of the holy: it is independent being that maintains its own identity – or integrity – intact over time. But the Western tradition has also acknowledged, of course, that everything that is in time is embedded in the causal nexus, and is therefore subject to continual change. It seems, then, that our traditional ideas about substance and identity are not compatible with our ideas about time, change and causality. Why did we ever allow ourselves to get stuck with this contradiction? Answer: because we somehow couldn't bear the flux. We hated the suggestion that there is ultimately nothing but an endless dance of phenomena, seemings. We felt that we must struggle to define and maintain clear boundaries and distinct identities. Once again we see that the central ideas and arguments of philosophy are the ghosts of older religious ideas and problems.

The second point concerns the human life of Christ. As the New Testament acknowledges, the corpse of a condemned man who had suffered public execution was a very unclean object indeed. I don't think the point was much discussed before the later Middle Ages, but it is very clear to Grünewald, Luther, Calvin, Holbein and others in their day that for our sakes Jesus Christ the Son of God Incarnate has suffered radical defilement. How was this possible, and what are we to make of it?

When we approach the question of the death of Christ from our present angle, we see that for Christians with a strong understanding *both* of the Incarnation *and* of the traditional religious notion of holiness, the manner of Christ's death made it a subject of unbearable horror. We see now why the Crucifixion was not a popular topic in first-millennium art, and why there is to this day no canonical 'doctrine of the Atonement'. All early theories of the Atonement do more to express bafflement than to shed light. Some, including the prophet Muhammad, found the Crucifixion so religiously unthinkable that they ended by saying that it could not have happened.[2] Something rather similar was said by all those early Fathers who treated the Crucifixion as a *deception*, a trick by which God has outwitted the Devil. Others produced an equally far-fetched account of the Crucifixion as a cosmic sacrifice, forgetting that 'sacrifice', as the word implies, involves a *consecration* of the Victim, whereas here we are talking about the Victim's radical *defilement*. How can the radical defilement of the Holiest of All be anything else but the most nihilistic of all ideas, the event that destroys everything? Some (such as Anselm, in *Cur*

Deus Homo) imagine a tragic conflict in God between the inexorable demand of his justice and the boundlessness of his mercy, a conflict that can only be resolved by Christ's death in this manner. For Anselm's sake I am glad that he could not see what he is on the brink of saying here: namely, that the tragic conflict in God between his inexorable Holy justice and his boundless mercy cuts so deep that it can be resolved only by the Death of God.

Only in a later period, the period of Luther and Calvin, the period of Mathias Grünewald's *Isenheim Altarpiece* (1515) and Holbein's *Dead Christ* (the 1520s), does it at last begin to be seen and said more clearly that the death of Christ really is also and conclusively the Death of God. But that thought took centuries to become fully explicit. It will be a while yet before we are able to say that in the first millennium God-centred church-Christianity grew and flowered; and then during the second millennium Christ-centred church-Christianity grew and developed towards religious humanism. The Church became monstrously oppressive and overblown as it made an idol of itself; but its saving grace was that it preserved in its central symbol, the Crucifixion, an image of its own ultimate and necessary self-cancellation. And at the end of the second millennium, as church-Christianity died, we at last became able to see in the dead Christ the meeting of pure nihility and pure humanism out of which the kingdom-religion of the third millennium will grow.

I should mention here the beautiful Mahayana Buddhist maxim that enjoins us to 'cling to the void and practise compassion'. As so often, Buddhism thinks and speaks more clearly, but Christianity has the more overwhelming and numinously-powerful imagery. Looking at the Crucifix, dying with Christ, we confront the Nihil and learn to love the human. It is so utterly light and fleeting, but it's all we have and all there is for us.

Chapter Four

The Coming of Immediate Religion

I have been working out one instance of a general thesis: we need to think of reforming, not just the Church and not just the Creed, but Christianity itself, because in late-modern times we have experienced the breakdown of many deep assumptions that have hitherto underlain almost all of religious and philosophical thought.

The example taken so far is this, that developed 'catholic' church-Christianity, from the late second century to the early twentieth century, was heavily influenced by the return of very ancient ideas about holiness and pollution. These ideas not only made Christianity a predominantly celibate religion which constructed elaborate scales of degrees of holiness of various persons, seasons and places, but they also had everyone thinking that there is something religiously unclean about the normal functioning of the female reproductive apparatus – and continuing to think in this way *until within living memory*. These ideas cut deep, and it is shocking to realise the extent to which they still influence us. A holy person, the kind of person you should try to become, is still an anxious person, someone who shrinks or recoils from full involvement in the to and fro of life because she or he fears defilement by 'the world'. To *mix in* is to risk impurity. These ideas were so powerful that they dominated Christian art, and made it impossible for Christians to imagine either Jesus or his mother as having been normal human beings. Mary in Christian art is the ultimate doormat: with the exception of her cousin Elizabeth, she cannot look any other adult person in the eye. She lives only to care for, and especially to *suffer* for her child. And Jesus is equally odd and distorted. The Jesus of art is the Jesus of piety, a passive, silent figure and quite unlike the Jesus of the Synoptic Gospels, who is highly disputatious, pure trouble. You can't imagine Jesus 'going to church' and sitting quietly in the congregation: on the contrary, every time he turns up there is a row. The one exception is the hilarious occasion on the evening of Palm Sunday: Jesus makes for the Temple, but it is already dusk. The place is emptying; it's too late to start anything (Mark 11:11). Disconcerted, he leaves – but next day he more than makes up for the previous day's anticlimax. (Matthew and Luke are so discomfited by the suggestion that Jesus had once entered the Temple without being able to cause any serious trouble that they cut the episode out.) But alas, the vehemence and argumentativeness of Jesus simply does not get through into Christian art. In art, as in St John's Gospel, his zest for conflict is missing. He never really *mixes it* with others: a really holy person cannot be thought of as *mixing it*, because mixture equals pollution. What is holy has to be kept separate. In Christian art, Jesus is nearly always standing back and looking silent, reproachful and a little sad. He has to go through with it, and does so; but he's not enjoying it much. In the Synoptic Gospels he is consciously *not* an ascetic like John the Baptist: he 'comes eating and drinking', so much so that his critics sniff at him for 'a gluttonous man and a winebibber'. But in Christian art he does not come across as one who loves life. Indeed, Christian art generally is not life affirming, but 'solemn' and otherworldly. It seems that the Jesus of the Synoptic Gospels was always too much for Christians, so they traded him in for the rather introverted and 'idealized' Jesus of Christian art. The truth is that coming to be thought of as God Incarnate *diminished* Jesus very severely. It took all the life out of him.

Then not very long ago, and perhaps as recently as the 1960s, the old notion of the Holy suddenly collapsed, and the old notions of pollution – and especially of menstruation and childbirth as creating states of ritual impurity – became unendurable and we actively dismissed them. By the 1980s I was aware that people in general had lost all feeling for holy places and holy persons. One simply does not *feel* that kind of sacred awe and dread any longer. The Sacred as a distinct sphere of life has now been swallowed entire by the tourist industry and converted into 'heritage'. It is a foreign country, lost in the past. We seek it out, hoping for an aftertaste of it, and wondering what sort of negligence it can have been that caused us suddenly to lose something so great and so unmistakable – but also, so utterly repugnant.

The answer to this puzzle is that the Holy has not simply vanished. What has happened is rather that the holy has become diffused and scattered across the whole human life world. The novel replaces theology: the religious realm is now not a second, distinct world, but is simply the world of 'life'. Tolstoy's *War and Peace*, written during the mid-1860s when the author was at the height of his powers, is the single most important early witness (unless one counts Wordsworth, perhaps?) to the new religious sense of 'life':

> Life is everything. Life is God. Everything changes and moves to and fro, and that movement is God. And while there is life there is joy in consciousness of the Godhead. To love life is to love God.[1]

Now, if it is true that the distinction between Sacred and Profane realms — once seemingly constitutive of religion — has recently vanished, then we must recognize that it has carried away with it a number of other basic features of religion. The first is the notion of *a hidden supernatural world* or spirit world, alongside the visible world. The denizens of the spirit world, namely God or the gods, spirits, and saints, are very holy and powerful beings who in varying degrees control events in the visible world. The second basic feature of traditional religion is *doctrine*: vitally important beliefs about the spirit world and our relations with the spirits have been revealed to us, and are handed down to us by tradition. And the third feature of traditional religion is *ritual*: we need to worship, and we need to do business with the spirit beings. The correct symbolic behavioural language for communicating with the spirits is prescribed by holy tradition.

The chief business of religion as we have known it hitherto, I am suggesting, was with *a supernatural world* of gods and spirits: one had to hold the correct, authoritatively validated credal beliefs about it, and one had to perform the correct, traditionally prescribed rituals when doing business with it. But we find that in modern Western culture the holy is no longer concentrated in a distinct religious sphere, but has become diffused all over the lifeworld. Various nineteenth-century writers saw this event coming, but I have argued elsewhere that it has become *demonstrably* embedded in ordinary language and in everyone's life experience only during the last forty years or so.[2] Its arrival signals the end of the mediated, church type Christianity that we have known hitherto. If they are to survive at all, creed and ritual must take a very different form.

All is not lost, however. Traditional Christianity was well aware that Jesus himself had preached the coming *on this earth* of a new age of immediate religion, which he called 'the Kingdom of God'. In his parables and sayings the content of his message was notably *this* worldly. However he did not see the Kingdom arrive, and after his martyrdom its coming still seemed to be delayed, and the quasi-military, disciplinary religious organisation of church Christianity evolved as a stopgap. Eventually, it was hoped, Jesus would return and the Kingdom would at last come on earth. Liberal Christianity further sharpened up the contrast between the kingdom religion of Jesus and church Christianity by emphasizing the gulf between 'the Jesus of history' and 'the Christ of faith', and by being ready even to put the original Jesus firmly outside 'Christianity'. Modern students of the Gospels are familiar with the idea that Jesus did *not* come to teach doctrines about himself. Indeed, he was not really a *doctrinal* teacher at all. He did not 'claim to be God', and in his public teaching at least he did not personally claim the Messiahship. He has little to say about the supernatural order. He did not 'found the Church', he did not commission the Church's ministry, and he did not literally 'institute the sacraments'. He was a Jewish exorcist and teacher, a prophet of the Kingdom of God and a controversial critic of mediated religion. The Church's attempt posthumously to make him into both the foundation and the founder of the Church, the ministry, the sacraments and the ecclesiastical Faith has had the effect of disastrously obscuring his own message, which was something very different and much more interesting. And the obscuring of the original Jesus was then further compounded by the canonization of St John's Gospel. But now, as the whole church system fades, Jesus at last begins to re-emerge and can be seen more clearly. For him, the religious life is the moral life – 'humanitarian ethics' – lived with what I might call 'solar fury', and others might call intense eschatological urgency. One should be unconditionally committed to life in its very transience; even in its very nihility. One should live as if at the end of the world, with the furious joy of those insects that have only one or two days to emerge, dry out their wings, sip a little nectar, find a mate, copulate energetically, lay their eggs and die. One has a work to do and one must do it in a hurry, with furious joy.

Another religious assumption, closely bound up with the ones already discussed and also needing today to be questioned, is the assumption that religion is the concern for the invisible spirit world that surrounds us. The spiritual realm was regarded as being sacred and highly authoritative. Its denizens are immortals and of great power. Everything in the everyday world has its archetypal counterpart in the spirit world. From the spirit world everything in the empirical world is created, grounded, legitimated and controlled. It is vital to our well-being that we should acknowledge and get on good terms with this invisible world. Religion exists to tell us all about the spirit world and to tell us how to worship – worship being a symbolic communication system through which we can do business with the spirits. In worship we use special forms that have been taught us by God, the gods or the spirits: this is how they want us to address them. Now so long as people really thought like this, worship remained an intelligible and important activity. But today immanentist ways of thinking have made such extraordinary progress in many spheres (history, biology, language, etc.) that the whole idea of a second world being needed to support this world and hold it together has become completely redundant. Again, 'life' is an outsideless continuum. And if so, what is the point of worship? There are of course stars who are worshipped and fans who worship them; but in our experience worship does not do much good either to the one who is worshipped or to the devotee. Can we drop the idea of worship: can we imagine religion without worship? And can we imagine religion becoming completely naturalistic and life centred, while yet remaining truly religion? If we can, we will say that religion is not now about the way we relate ourselves to the supernatural realm: religion is about the way we relate ourselves to 'life'.

A third religious assumption: until recently most or nearly all religions were systems of mediation. In order to get yourself into the right relationship to God or the gods you must go through all the proper channels; and that meant that you must read the right scriptures, believe exactly the right creed, use just the right Names for the Holy Ones you worship, join the right religious community, get yourself into communion with the right Pontiff (*pontifex* means 'bridgemaker') and so on. The sheer number and the burdensomeness of all these proper channels or bridges to the divine is so great that there has of course been a long history of attempts to circumvent them and find a direct way to God through mysticism, through charismatic gifts and through religious enthusiasm and ecstasies. But nobody has yet found an easy way to *stabilize* religious immediacy. It flares up, and it dies away again. We can't hold it steady, and the usual view has been that we must defer any security in it until after death. So we have tended to fall back on the view that in this life we must simply put up with mediated religion, and must accept the myths (Christ's Commission to Peter, Christ's Institution of the Eucharist, etc.) that it invokes in support of its own legitimacy.

Today however – and I think the point scarcely needs arguing – we cannot help but be aware of how rusty and oppressive is the elaborate machinery of mediated religion, how naïve are its exclusive claims, and how exploded are the various myths of origin or institution narratives that are recited in its support. These things cannot be believed in any more, and we need to find ways of doing without them.

Two or three philosophical assumptions that we need to learn to do without may now be mentioned. The first is metaphysical realism, the belief that we are presented with a ready-made real world, a cosmos whose reality and intelligible order are determined from a point that is both outside ourselves, and also outside and beyond the here and now. Instead, the philosophies of Kant and Hegel have very gradually accustomed us to the idea that the reality of all things is presented to us in the here and now, *in our knowledge of them*, and that the real world is therefore not a timeless world, but is historically developing. This point is so astoundingly simple that I am frantic about my own twenty year failure to get it across to my own generation; but I'm saying only that Real-ization is taking place *now*, through *us*, for us. We have come to the end of a very ancient notion of reality as metaphysically mediated to us and pre-established for us, and have arrived at an age of immediacy. There is no longer any call to look Beyond: it's all happening here and now before your very eyes. Everything takes shape and becomes itself in your seeing of it. It's all yours, as *you make it* **out**. All this is all there is. No spirit world or transcendent entity mediates the real to us. *We* order the world. Real-ization is the historical process, and we are the actors. It all happens in us, through us. And it is because we have come at last to a post-metaphysical age of immediacy that religion has to go immediate *too*, and the old clanking belief-based, mediated and ecclesiastical sort of religion is currently giving place at last to the immediate, 'Kingdom' sort of religion that Jesus preached, but didn't live to see.

A second philosophical assumption is the old belief in objective truth, or rather truths, truths that have come into the world and are handed down from generation to generation without any change. Both rationalists and moralists are deeply attached to the idea of objective, timeless (and usually 'traditional') truth. Catholics talk about the immutability of dogma, and Protestants talk of the Gospel as belonging to and being about Jesus Christ, who is 'the same yesterday, today and forever'. In a changing world many people feel that unchanging, objective, ready-made truths are like firm bars or handrails that they can grip in order to help themselves stay upright. But we have to give up this idea. It misunderstands the nature and the place of truth. The locus of truth is the place of Real-ization, the place where in us Being comes forth into language and everything takes shape. The locus of truth is not quite in language only and not quite in be-ing only, but at the point where the two meet – a point which is always now, and always changing. Truth has to be *lived*; it has to be remade, reimagined, rethought, all the time. So we come again from another angle to the recognition that the older mediated kind of religion, belief in dogmatic Truths, is currently giving way to a new kind of religious immediacy, truth in life. Living truth, truth in process.

A third and last philosophical assumption, and a rather delicate one, is essentialism – the belief in fixed, objective, defining essences of things. This is a belief that has played a large part in religion, and especially in religious controversy, where people fight over definitions and over who is or is not entitled to trade under a particular label or brand name. The matter causes many people much anxiety: they ask what is the essence of Christianity, and is someone who believes, or does not believe, this or that entitled to call herself a Christian? People feel anxiously that lines must be drawn somewhere, and worry about which side of the line they themselves may be found to be standing on. But I reply that all debates of this kind are merely political jostling and point scoring. There are no real essences out there, just as there aren't any fixed and compulsory meanings of words. Because of the way history goes, meanings and (supposed) essences are changing all the time. Words mean what we currently use them to mean, and things are what we currently take them for. And I say all this because a time of major religious change is of course also a time of sectarian squabbling over who's entitled to fly certain colours; and we must not allow ourselves to be misled and distracted by it. In fact, we won't be able to get to immediate religion, and we won't be able to understand it, until we have entirely given up essentialism. While religion is mediated, there are sharp battles over whose system of mediation is the original and authentic one; but when we pass over into immediate religion we move into a region where all is utterly familiar and nameless. Labels are no longer needed. They no longer mean a thing. So although this book bears the title *Reforming Christianity*, people will of course say that the kingdom religion I describe is 'not Christianity' – and we must of course be utterly indifferent to that charge, because it is based on an obsolete assumption.

Chapter Five

Kingdom Religion

W
hat will the theology of a reformed Christianity look like? I have already said that in the process of its reformation Christianity has to move on from its ecclesiastical period, its 'schooldays', now ending, to its fully adult form, the 'kingdom religion' that Jesus originally lived, preached and hoped to see on earth.

In *Kingdom Come in Everyday Speech* I sketched the difference between the ecclesiastical type of theology we've known hitherto, and the new kingdom theology:

> Here then is a brief checklist of the principal points of difference between ecclesiastical theology and kingdom theology. *First*, in ecclesiastical theology the whole world of the here and now is subordinated to a greater and better World Beyond, whereas in kingdom theology there is no Beyond at all. All is arrival, victory, and rest in the here and now.
>
> Most of the other contrasts are related to this first one. Thus, and *secondly*, in ecclesiastical religion God is transcendent, Other, and unknown, whereas in kingdom religion God is wholly immanent. *Thirdly*, ecclesiastical religion is mediated by authoritative scriptures, creeds, rituals and priests, whereas kingdom religion is immediate and intuitive. *Fourthly*, in ecclesiastical religion credal, dogmatic faith is a *sine qua non*, whereas kingdom religion is visionary and beliefless. There being no unseen beyond, dogmatic faith is not needed. The reason why one lives *after belief* is the same as the reason why one lives *after history*: one is no longer aspiring after or waiting for anything unseen that one does not already have. *Fifthly*, in ecclesiastical theology there is much emphasis upon rank, hierarchy and inequalities, whereas kingdom theology is highly egalitarian and knows nothing of titles or degrees of rank. Ecclesiastical theology is popish, and kingdom theology is quakerish. *Sixthly*, ecclesiastical theology canonizes

one particular vocabulary, a particular cultural tradition and particular lineages of teaching authority, whereas kingdom theology has forgotten tradition and is at last fully 'ecumenical' or globalized – i.e., catholic or pan-ethnic.

Generalizing, and *seventhly*, one may say that in the ecclesiastical world great importance is attached to the fact that much is mysterious, dark, latent, deferred, unseen and generally beyond our ken, whereas in the kingdom everything is explicit, out in the open, equally lit and plain, with no darkness or shadows at all. People are entirely transparent to each other. So also and *eighthly*, whereas the ecclesiastical world is a world of many languages, of pluralism and discord, the kingdom world is a world of one equal music. And *finally*, in ecclesiastical culture a clear and very important distinction is made between the sacred and profane realms, whereas in the kingdom the sacred/profane distinction is simply not made. Or we may say if we wish that the common speech of plain people is itself the only sacred language.

A corollary of kingdom theology's eschewal of the sacred/profane distinction is that it does not need and does not make the traditional distinction between Church and State. The religious community, insofar as it exists at all as a distinct body, is described simply as a society of friends.[1]

The contrast made here, between the present less than satisfactory religious setup (ecclesiastical theology) and an ideal future one (kingdom theology) is deeply rooted in the Bible. All the way through, the principal theme is a hope that one day the present cumbrous apparatus of religious authority and religious mediation will no longer be necessary, and religion will at last become fully democratized.

> . . . But this is the covenant which I will make with the house of Israel after those days, says the LORD: I will put my law within them and I will write it upon their hearts; and I will be their God, and they shall be my people. And no longer shall each man teach his neighbour and each his brother, saying, 'Know the LORD', for they shall all know me from the least of them to the greatest, says the LORD; for I will forgive their iniquity, and I will remember their sin no more.[2]

People's relation to God will no longer be dominated either by the need to be assured of forgiveness for their sins, or by a disciplinary system of religious Law, taught and enforced by a large class of religious professionals. Instead religion will become easy and spontaneous. It will be the way all people 'naturally' relate themselves to life.

The idea of religious democratization is by no means unique to the Hebrew Bible and later traditions influenced by it. On the contrary, it is a widespread feature of the history of religions – including even the religion of ancient Egypt. The commonest pattern is that a special relation to the god, which originally belonged only to the King, comes gradually to be claimed and enjoyed by a wider and wider circle of people until eventually it reaches everyone.

In the case of Christianity there are a number of special complications and strains. Jesus preached the Kingdom; but what we got was the church, which over a dozen or so centuries developed into the most spectacular, highly differentiated and cruelly persecuting system of religious mediation that there has ever been. It made a great idol of itself: people became incurably in love with it even as it irremediably damaged them – which still happens. And one way you could write second-millennium church history would be as the story of the endless conflict between those who always seek to build up the system of mediation and strengthen its terrible power over the hapless individual believer, and those on the other hand who have always struggled to weaken the system's grip by finding ways of bypassing the proper channels and attaining religious happiness directly (as in mysticism, Protestantism, and charismatic and pentecostal Christianity), or by arguing that we have already come to the end of the historical epoch dominated by the church, and may now move on to the kingdom era (the Radical Reformation, the Society of Friends, the Kingdom of God in America, the Coming-of-Age of Man, and now Postmodern Postchristianity).

It is certainly arguable that the battle here has been going on almost without a break not merely since Thomas Münzer in the 1520s, but even since the twelfth century, the age of the Franciscans and of Joachim of Fiore (1132–1200). In a word, the battle has gone on for so long that it perhaps reflects a permanent tension within Christianity itself between order and freedom – between, that is, the need in any historical society for standard symbols, rituals and disciplinary structures, and the clamour of those who will always try to argue that we have now outgrown the need for such structures and can escape into pure spiritual freedom. And if this is true, then my own thesis gets trapped again within the history that it struggles to escape. 'Now is the time when we can at last try to escape from the stifling limitations of church Christianity', I say – and back comes the weary reply: 'Familiar stuff. We've always understood that in every age there will be some impatient people like you who can't put up with the long hard slog of church history. You want to jump the gun. You want to seize perfection prematurely: but history shows that people like you always come to a very sticky end.' So whatever I say can have no effect: the system has seen it all before. Whatever we say about kingdom theology has already been allowed for and slotted away.

There is a further complication: some vital elements of kingdom religion were from early times appropriated into the infant ecclesiastical faith. They were the pentecostal gift of the Spirit by which God becomes distributed into people and wholly immanent, and the Eucharist, a fellowship meal that Jesus himself had reportedly assigned expressly to the Kingdom.[3] The fact that the church has already incorporated certain features of the kingdom (while taking care to reinterpret them in its own interest) explains why the church does have a strand in its language and in its self-understanding that claims that it already *is* the kingdom – being realized in slow motion, perhaps – and that it can readily tolerate the use of kingdom language and the living of the kingdom lifestyle within itself (provided of course that one is suitably discreet in one's language, and does not upset the authorities).

All this threatens to leave me badly outmanoeuvred. I cannot get any leverage or purchase upon the church, when it claims already to know and already to have assimilated everything in the way of strictly *theological* argument that I can bring forward against it. For if I say that the huge apparatus of religious mediation is religiously oppressive and badly outdated, and that we should now abandon it and move on quickly to the next and long awaited phase in Christianity's historical development, namely kingdom religion, then the church can smile indulgently and point out all the evidence that – in a hidden way – it already *is* the kingdom. But the kingdom's full manifestation is unfortunately still delayed, so in the interim the church tells us that we must stay with her. Not least, because all ordinary people think that the great apparatus of mediation – the Church, the Bible, the Creeds, the Sacraments, the Ministry, Canon Law and the rest – all that is the very *substance* of Christianity. It is indeed officially 'necessary to salvation'. And ordinary believers do not see the great apparatus of orthodoxy as something transitional and very imperfect that we long to be delivered from. In their eyes it is the real thing and they regard kingdom theology as *reductionist!* Not something far greater, but something *less*. So for their sakes we must cling to mediated religion. It is all they know, and in any case it has already assimilated something of the kingdom, and does still point forward to the kingdom. It may not be as finally right as they think it is, but neither is it wholly wrong. It will get them there in the end.

The reader will see that I have somewhat modified the classical apologia of the Grand Inquisitor, and I admit that in the form just presented, it undercuts me. However bad things get for the church, it will still not be persuaded by my historicist argument, from traditional theological premises, for a new Reformation. The church has always known that it is supposed to be only a transitional arrangement, and has known for at least a hundred years that orthodox doctrine is not really scriptural, and that it gets Jesus badly wrong. But ordinary people firmly believe that ecclesiastical orthodoxy is true Christianity, and indeed the church does contain a few elements of kingdom religion and does still look forward to the kingdom. So it will always seem 'wiser' to hang on to the status quo for a while longer. 'Lord, give us a new reformation', says every bishop, 'but not in *my* time, please, not in my time. Thy kingdom come, but not just yet'.

From all this I conclude that I will not be able to get far enough by a purely theological defence of kingdom theology. Our religious tradition is very dispensational, in a way that makes religious truth relative to the 'dispensation', or epoch, that one takes oneself to be living in. For example, in the period of 'the Law' God is relatively very distinct and vivid; in the New Testament and ecclesiastical period God steadily turns into Christ and gives himself into human beings; and in the kingdom period God is 'spirit', completely returned into and immanent in the flux of 'life' and the to-and-fro of human relationships. But epochs can overlap, and there is often room for argument about just how to characterize one's own time. We have, after all, felt ourselves to be living in a time of transition for the past *three centuries*. And what makes things more awkward still is the awareness that my argument for a move into kingdom theology may in its turn be trumped by Muslims who argue that Islam is itself already the Kingdom of God on earth, and the true successor of Christian ecclesiastical theology.

We therefore need to make clear what kind of truth we attribute to kingdom theology, and how we propose to establish it. I have accepted that I cannot fully vindicate kingdom theology by conventional theological argument, mainly because of the ambiguities and uncertainties that must surround any attempt to characterize the theological status of our own time and to argue that the revolutionary moment has come, just *now*. And we have already noted earlier that we are dispensing with two ideas that are very prominent in ecclesiastical theology, namely the ideas of revelation and dogmatic truth. So what form can my apologetics take?

Two slogans that have already been introduced elsewhere give the answer to this: They are *Ordinary language already presupposes kingdom theology*, and the phrase, *Philosophy's own religion*.

That in the thought of both Kant and Hegel there is a certain movement from ecclesiastical theology to kingdom theology is well known; but in the three short Everyday Speech books I have pointed out recently that ordinary language today already has built into it, already presupposes, much of the world view and values of kingdom theology. God is dispersed into the movement and the claims of 'life', and ordinary language seeks a world that is fully appropriated to humanity:

> . . . ordinary language posits and aspires after a 'kingdom-world' – a purely human, moral world like the kingdom of God in the Bible, or Kant's kingdom of ends. Language developed for the sake of human networking. . . . Ordinary language therefore looks for a world of unfettered and mutually transparent human communication, in which everything non-human that encircles us and threatens us – **it all** – is either chained up or at least deferred or kept at bay. Language's own philosophy is a form of radical humanism, and its politics is democratic. Reality is or should be made a network of persons whose impersonal environment sustains, but does not distort, their free converse with each other.
>
> [We go on to ask] how far in ordinary language today the traditional religious eschatology has been 'realised', or made actual in the present age. If indeed ordinary language has brought heaven and hell forward, so that they have become states of affairs or states of mind that are readily accessible to people now, what are the implications? Are we already living in post-history, in the world at the end of the world that has no further world lying beyond it? The answer seems to be Yes: ordinary language's basic cosmological distinction is no longer that between God and the created order, including Man, but that between the human world and the encircling non-human. Ordinary language seems to picture Christianity as having already moved into its post-ecclesiastical and final stage of development.[4]

– and our own world, which is increasingly globalized, humanitarian and ultra-communicative, is still struggling to realise humankind's ancient hopes, and become itself the long awaited kingdom world.

A crucial factor in all this is the end of belief in life after death. When I force myself to confront the fact that my coming death really will be my simple extinction, I really do begin to see this present world as the last world, and this life, in its very lightness and transience, as being religiously final. The End is near: it really is. In our time, ordinary life has a touch of eschatological urgency about it. Everyone is aware that we live only once, and that death and nothingness are only a heartbeat away. The human means everything to us, but it is desperately fragile.

In such a context, kingdom theology is nothing exotic or fanciful. It is presupposed by our ordinary language *now*. It is what we already perceive to be the truth about our life *now*. And it is also *philosophy's own religion*. For in systematic philosophy, when we try to say how it is now with us human beings and our world and how we should live, we come up with a vision of things that comes to a very sharp edge where nihilism meets humanism. We are thoroughgoing anti-realists, to the point of nihilism. Apart from us the world is an Empty flux, which language struggles to form, to differentiate, and to appropriate, so that we human beings can become ourselves as we recognize our world and each other. I argue then for anti-realist philosophy, with 'solar' personal ethics and humanitarian social ethics, and the whole philosophy is a form of radical humanism rather like that expressed in traditional religious visions of the heavenly world: the real is – or should be constructed as – a network of fully reconciled and mutually transparent persons. Kingdom theology again.

Thus, for me (and in ways that have been spelt out more fully elsewhere[5]) kingdom theology is an interpretation of our own human condition that I am led to by philosophy, and kingdom religion is a form of religious response to life that I find to be *true to* our own times. Since our modern Western culture remains deeply influenced by Christianity, it is not at all surprising that Christianity's founding vision of a better world is still today shaping our hopes and influencing the way we are building our world.

This makes clear what I can and cannot argue. I cannot, I concede, expect to succeed in developing, within ecclesiastical theology and on its own terms, an argument that will push the Church into reforming itself beyond itself and into the kingdom. But I can argue, and have argued, that kingdom theology is the *truth of* our own times, and that kingdom religion (i.e. 'solar' spirituality, *plus* humanitarian social ethics) is the form of religious life that is *true to* our own times. That is, you may protest, a very queer sort of argument for the truth of (a version of) Christianity; but I am deliberately presenting here a new sort of apologetic that does not appeal to tradition, or to authority, and does not propose any supernatural beliefs, but merely tries to show how it currently is with us.

Chapter
Six

Outside In

I n the old Christian culture that was dominated by the Church, most people drew their basic picture of the world and the human condition from Christian doctrine – and that meant the great doctrines of Creation, the Fall and Redemption, all understood in a strongly realistic way. The resulting world picture was at once highly optimistic and highly moralistic. In the beginning God had created each of us for himself. He was all-wise and all-good, and the cosmic order that he had originally established was like an idealized patriarchal household. Everything was designed for a purpose, everything was arranged in a balanced and harmonious order, and everything was carefully watched over. Unfortunately, very soon after the original creation of human beings, human sin had begun to disturb and to corrupt the intended perfect balance of things, and all of human life had come to be blighted by limitation, by labour and suffering and by sin. We no longer deserve the happiness for which we were made: on the contrary, we deserve only damnation. But fortunately God has prepared a remedy through which he will restore at least some human beings to their original high destiny, and the cosmic order to its original harmony and perfection. What is this remedy, and how will it work? The best way to answer this great question is by reciting the long history of salvation that culminates in the Incarnation, the atoning death, the Resurrection and Ascension and now the heavenly session of the Son of God in Jesus Christ our Lord. Out of these events has come the Church, which through its Creed, its disciplines and its Sacraments mediates eternal salvation to us. In this life most of us cannot expect to have more than a promise of the glory that is to come, but we may draw encouragement from the holy lives of his saints, from the miracles that are still part of the

41

life of the Church, and from our own experience of sacramental grace. If we die in a state of grace and in the true faith, we may hope at last to have a part in the full glory that awaits the redeemed in Heaven.

In retrospect this seems a strange world picture, and in view of the extreme harshness of life for the peasantry before modern times, one may wonder why it was so widely and so long believed. Surely, the ordinary person's experience of life did not offer much confirmation of it all? In reply one may say that the whole scheme of thought did at least make human sense of the world. It promised the peasant that the highest authority of all is wise and good, and warned him or her that to a great extent they had only themselves (and all their ancestors) to blame for their own misfortunes. Yet if they will but believe the Church's teaching, submit, conform and endure to the end, they can hope for a glory almost beyond imagination that awaits them after death.

It is notable that on this whole account religion is seen in terms of ecstatic passivity in one's reception of overwhelmingly great theological facts. God has determined and will continue to determine everything by his infinite power. Our proper response has two chief components: worship and obedience. And that is all: the realism with which doctrine is understood, and the infinite difference between God's power and ours, leave no room for human beings to make any active contribution either to their own redemption, or to the world's restoration.

I need hardly say that the principal objection to the old Christian cosmology is that it is simply wrong.[1] If we know anything at all about the world, we know that it is not run in that way. If the way things go is law governed, then the hidden rules are perhaps mechanical, perhaps stochastic, or perhaps a bit of both; but at least we can be sure that *they are not moral*. That is to say, they are not the rules of any morality that has been revealed to us.

So let us try instead an entirely different way of interpreting Christian doctrine. This time, let us begin with what in the twenty-first century we know to be the truth about the human condition, and then ask what use religious ideas might be found to have in that context.

The truth of the human condition, then, is pretty much as it is presented by Samuel Beckett. There is not 'literally' any God out there. There is no life after death: the end of our life is simply the end of our life, as we all know. There is no antecedently laid on or ready-made cosmic order out there, nor any moral order either. There isn't even any ready-made self, and there is no ready-made Meaning of Life.

Only two things are given: we are given the temporal flow of life, bringing to us the disorderly tumult of sense experience and our varying feeling response to it: and secondly, we are given, from as far back as memory or analysis can reach, the beginnings of language, which starts to turn the stream of experiences and feelings into a stream of signs, verbal and other. The words themselves don't at first make much sense: they may be little better than babble or delirium. In the beginning one is not sure even of the ability to tell sense from nonsense.

I am saying, you will gather, that so far as there is something called the human condition that can be described truthfully, the theatre of Samuel Beckett describes it. He is inevitably too optimistic, for in his theatre he already has a stage, real actors, and the English and French languages in place. But take those away, and the impression that the texts make upon us is about right. Nihilism? Yes. That's where we are. And what use might it be possible to make of Christian doctrine in this situation?

This time, we don't see Christian doctrine as giving a true *description* of the world and the human condition. We see it as showing us *what we can do*. For it shows us *God* as facing up to the Nihil, the dark and formless primal condition of everything. *God* calls upon language as his weapon for overcoming nihilism. By his utterance *God* draws great lines across the Void, delimiting the major cosmic regions. His language differentiates things:

> He determines the number of the stars,
> He gives to all of them their names.
>   – Ps 147:4

So God's language establishes an ordered cosmos and assigns to everything its name and its value. In this way, God does the same job as is done in some other mythologies by the tribal ancestor: his action is archetypal. He does everything for the first time and shows us how we too are to conquer nihilism and build an ordered and value rich world around ourselves. Interestingly, God in Genesis allows the man, Adam, a small part in his own archetypal work of creation by calling upon Adam to name the beasts. The reason for this is presumably that in the very earliest times the hunting and then the successful domestication of animals was the prime and the chief example of human technical power over nature.

Already the main theme of this alternative story about how to read Christian mythology is emerging: it is the *imitatio Dei*, the mimicking of God — a theme not unknown within the ecclesiastical tradition, but usually played down. Church Christianity operated within a strongly realistic framework of thought that projected Christian myth out as a vast and overpowering ideology of domination, with the cosmos all readymade and all the authorities in Church and the State already established. Because everything was seen as being readymade out there, the ordinary person's creativity was usually denied: it was not your business to *imitate* God, but merely to respond fittingly to what he had done. That meant passively accepting your readymade slot in the whole divinely ordained scheme of things. Your part was to believe, to obey divine Law, to endure and to hope – and that was all. Thus 'Christianity' became organized as an antihumanist and oppressive cultural system, which to some extent it still remains. To this day any notable technical advance, especially in medicine, is liable to be greeted with accusations that scientists or doctors are 'playing God', as if somehow we all just *know* that playing God is a bad thing to do. Only God is allowed to play God, and he has already done it to the full. This shows very clearly how strong the influence of ecclesiastical doctrine still is, and how completely it has forgotten what religious ideas are and how they work. For in religion, myths supply archetypal patterns that are *intended* to be reenacted in the lives of believers. You are *supposed* to play God, for God's sake! The creation myth is an archetypal story about how *we* by language must overcome the original formless chaos of experience and mental life, and gradually build and order our world and give it value. In short, if you are a literal theist then of course Christian doctrine is not true; but if you are a nihilist, then you can see that Christian doctrine is regulatively true for you. It is a true myth, for it shows you how to build and order your world. I have already indicated that in the myth God is pictured as an 'active non-realist' who uses language to build his world out of nothing; and we who today find ourselves in the same situation are to do the same.

With the same motive: in classical theology it was sometimes asked *why* God, who was already infinite and perfect and needed nothing, should have created a world. What had he to gain? The best answer available was that God had created the cosmos to be a theatre for his glory, out of sheer pleasure in self-expression and out of a generous self-giving love. These are touching ideas, but they are naively anthropomorphic in terms of the traditional metaphysical theism. What can have been their point? The new answer to this old question draws attention to their very anthropomorphism. It is a giveaway: *God himself is solar*! He lives by expressing himself; he pours himself out and he gives value to things, even seemingly worthless or wicked things, just by loving them. He delights in the whole tragi-comedy of life. And this shows that when we talk about God we should not suppose that we are talking metaphysics:

we are talking about the idea of God as a role model for human life and moral action. In which case the continuing story of Fall and Redemption should be re-read as a story of how human beings can lose touch with their own myths and fall into moral alienation, disorder and conflict; and how a generous outgoing and expressive love can redeem the world, *giving* what is nowadays called 'self-worth' to other people and things just by loving them, re-describing them, and upgrading them.[2]

In the myth, God is not subject to any independently existing moral Law. He creates the moral order by his own self-expression in language, which builds, orders and gives value to his world. And we are to do exactly the same: there is of course no antecedently established moral order out there to which we are subject. We start in a moral void, just as we start in ontological Emptiness. Our business, as symbolizers and language using beings, is to be *solar*: to pour ourselves out into expression, generating and ordering our world and giving value to it and to each other. The myth of redemption promises that a sufficiently solar and generous love can redeem or revalue not merely the ungodly but even the actively wicked.

From this example we see how the new reformation, which coincides with the transition from Church religion to Kingdom religion, is going to turn our received ideas and thinking outside in. As soon as it moved out of Aramaic and into a Greek-speaking world, early Christianity entered a slave society in which absolute monarchy was the usual form of government. Things did not get much better until the Enlightenment. It is hardly surprising that in such a context few people ever recognized the imaginative and emancipatory possibilities of Christian myths and symbols. All the emphasis was placed upon the political use of religion for the purpose of social control. Christian myth was systematized and objectified as dogma, made compulsory, understood realistically, and *projected out as cosmology*. Savage social discipline was sanctified by religion, and reinterpreted as schooling for salvation. The believer's attention was directed towards a beautiful imaginary sacred world which she glimpsed in worship and entered permanently after death.

Church Christianity of the old sort used Christian materials to create a stable sacred civilization with the strongest machinery of social control that could be established at that period. Today, the last faded relics of that order are finally slipping away in Eastern Europe.

In the new Kingdom religion there is no use of Christian symbols and myths to construct a disciplinary cosmology, nor to validate hierarchies of spiritual and temporal power. But we do not therefore discard

them altogether. Not at all: we simply restore them to their proper, emancipatory and religious use. Turned outside in, internalized within the ordinary human subject, the old myths become programming that helps us
to function as religious artists; that is, it shows us how and it helps us,
through our own expressive activity, to build and redeem our worlds.

We see now why we have to talk about 'reforming Christianity', and
about a major shift, a change of dispensation. For it is only when we have
fully understood how and why the old kind of Church Christianity is
simply untrue as cosmology and historically obsolete that we can pass
through Nietzsche and Beckett, through atheism and nihilism, and come
to a region where, to our astonishment, Christianity turns out to be true
after all. *Not* true as a cosmic ideology of social control, but true after all
as emancipatory, liberating *religion*.

I hope also that we see now why the leaders of what remains of
ecclesiastical Christianity have so little understanding of religion, what it
is and how it works. In order to rediscover religion we shall have to break
with the Church, and learn a quite different way of thinking. We have to
relearn what religion is and how it works to liberate us and help us to
build our own world.

Inside Out

When, during the long mediaeval period, the substance of Christianity was systematized and projected out as cosmology it created an all encompassing sacred civilization that surrounded the ordinary person. Everything was seen as ready-made out there, and there was little scope to do more than conform passively. Huge hierarchies of temporal and, still more, spiritual power pressed upon the believer, demanding a tithe of the fruits of the labour of his body and the entire allegiance of his soul. It is no wonder that church Christianity today still exists in a state of yearning nostalgia for its own past greatness: it still thinks in the old way and it still longs to become again what it once was.

In the transition to its kingdom form, Christianity finds itself undergoing a double change. It is turned outside in, so that it ceases to be cosmology and becomes instead a kind of interior programming that shapes the way the believer builds her world and constructs her life. That change took place in Protestantism; but by itself it is not enough. By itself, it may be doing no more than replace an external 'political' tyranny with an equally objectionable inner psychological tyranny. So in the process of internalization 'the Faith' needs also to lose its dogmatic, systematic and coercive character. It has to become a large vocabulary of symbolic and mythical materials that people feel free to utilize as they wish in constructing their own appropriate worlds, forms of selfhood and styles of life. In short, church Christianity both Catholic and Protestant was so preoccupied with questions of power and social control that it did not redeem people. It was predominantly disciplinary, and postponed redemption until after death.

Now we know for sure that there is no life after death. Redemption has to be delivered in this life. That means that Christianity has got to become an effective working religion *now*, and in this our only life: it has to become genuinely emancipatory and liberating. People have to find in Christianity a symbolic vocabulary, a collection of forms of self-expression, through which they can, each in her and his own way, at last become fully themselves and build the world they want to see. The church is not and never has been *itself* Christianity: it has so far been only a preparatory school, getting believers ready for the full implementation of Christianity which was to take place, it was hoped, either in the far off future or after death. Today, however, the preparatory school is rapidly winding down: this must surely be our last chance to attempt actually to realize Christianity on earth.

Some say that it might have been done, and should have been done, around 1820. The French Revolution had signalled the end of the old regime: Kant had proclaimed the coming-of-age of humanity and the Romantics had recovered the idea of creative and expressive living, 'living from the heart'. Schleiermacher and a few others were beginning to talk of the Christian task as building the Kingdom of God on earth. Utopian hopes had been raised and change seemed possible; but it did not happen then, just as it did not happen in the mid-1960s either. Is it now too late?

Perhaps it *is* too late: but I still want to think out and try to spell out what would be required. We may find that some at least of the changes needed are already coming about in an unlabelled, unconscious way, just by the ordinary processes of cultural development. I have suggested elsewhere that in our times people are spontaneously taking to the ardent emotive expressive style of living that I call 'solar', and to humanitarian ethics. Both of these are rooted in the teaching of Jesus, and are characteristic of kingdom religion. So maybe *we are* 'building the Kingdom of God on earth' without anybody either in the churches or out of them being aware that this is what is happening. Maybe the Christian programme is at least beginning to be implemented, albeit in an unconscious, unlabelled fashion. Maybe that is so, and maybe that it is quite good enough; for as Hegel noted more than once, the transition to kingdom religion may require us to give up the ugly proprietorial and exclusive attitude to truth that always goes with the use of trademarks and brand names. Perhaps the Kingdom of God cannot come until words like *God, Kingdom, Christ* and *Christian* have all gone out of use, and nobody is looking for a chance to reintroduce them.

The suggestion that we are perhaps already moving over to a highly democratized, expressivist and humanitarian culture of leisure is highly relevant to this book's main thesis. Many people will say that the reformation of Christianity that we envisage involves too great a revolution in thought and in culture. Christianity is surely nowadays much too small and weak to be capable of thinking so big. However, I have argued elsewhere that the historical unfolding of the Christian project has been continuing, unlabelled, in the mainstream of Western culture. *In the mainstream*, the culture has moved over to kingdom religion, albeit of a somewhat disorderly and unselfconscious kind. *The mainstream* knows all about liberal democracy, nihilism and humanitarianism; *the mainstream* knows all about how the quest for personal salvation nowadays takes the form of a quest for self-realization by self-expression. Much of what I'm asking for is already being done for me. All I have to do is make the mainstream more aware of the religious significance of developments to which it is already committed, and also persuade the ecclesiastical remnant to take a new and much more optimistic view of what is going on in the world outside.

One strand in these new developments is particularly hard to understand, namely the turning inside out of the self – the reversal of the self's typical flow. In ecclesiastical Christianity the self was taught to be relatively passive, receptive and 'feminine'. God did all the work, and the soul was enjoined to lie back and think of Heaven. The turn of the self from Appearance to Reality was introvertive. One's real life was one's 'inner' or 'spiritual' life.

So it was in the ecclesiastical period. But in postmodernity and in the Kingdom the natural movement of the self as it seeks fulfilment is abruptly reversed. It becomes extravertive. The self seeks to come out into expression. Only by self-outing can the self truly become itself. It passionately desires to have everything explicit, confessed, declared and out in the open. It regards the old 'closet' spirituality of hidden inwardness as a deception, a cover up.

The metaphysics of selfhood is quite different under the new conditions. In the ecclesiastical period the human being was an amphibian, a being designed for life in two distinct worlds. The core self, the soul, was a finite spiritual substance, naturally immortal and as such destined for God and the eternal world. But it was also the animating principle, the 'form', of the body, and this brought it into close contact with the passions and with the many solicitations that reach us from the external world through our senses. Life in this world can threaten the soul's well-being, and to get through it safely one needs to avoid occasions of sin, to discipline the body and the passions, and frequently to recollect oneself and allow the soul some deep refreshing draughts of its proper air.

Ecclesiastical Christianity was for most of its history a religion that ranked virginity higher than marriage and was highly otherworldly in its orientation. One withdrew from the social world in order to open oneself to God. The life of the body and this world was viewed with caution at best. But during the Enlightenment a much more this worldly outlook, and with it a new understanding of the self, gradually came to prevail. The most influential thinkers were Schopenhauer, Darwin, Nietzsche and Freud, and it is to them that we chiefly owe the notion of selfhood that is now dominant in the culture as a whole.

On this newer view the human being is a talking animal, a being in whom Nature is all the time getting turned into Culture. The life of the self is powered by a collection of biological drives, often somewhat at odds with each other, that struggle to get out into expression. If they cannot find satisfactory expression we will feel ill, and perhaps fall ill. Culture supplies a range of approved forms, or proper channels, of symbolic expression. Each person tends to seize upon the forms of expression through which he or she can most easily and most fully become him/herself, fulfilling both the biological drives and her own personal aspirations, whilst also fitting in along with others who have their own similar projects, and meeting the demands of culture. In late Modern and Postmodern times rising prosperity and better social administration have made it possible for society to offer the individual a much wider and more attractive range of forms of selfhood and lifestyles than was available in the past. Hence the shift from a disciplinary culture to a leisure culture, and from 'Church' to 'Kingdom' religion.

In the model I am proposing, then, the self works by an expressive outgoing movement. It seeks to come out. Libido, the life impulse, is a bundle of rather polymorphous, disorganized drives that struggle for expression. They want to get out into what Schopenhauer calls 'representation', and I'm calling symbolic expression. Culture supplies a range of permitted forms of expression: language, patterns of behaviour and so on. Our libido flows into and sets in motion the utterances and behaviours through which our often ambivalent feelings, can find their best, their fullest, most coherent and most meaningful expression. So we are continually expressing ourselves, and seeking to become ourselves *in passing*, as we pass out into expression and pass away. *In passing*, also, we are all the time communicating with others and building our common world.

Yes – the moment in which the flow of biological feeling fills a symbolic form (a word, or any other general sign) is the moment in which everything comes into Be-ing, or is Real-ized.

It happens in us all the time, before our very eyes. I urge the reader to look meditatively at the visual field, or to listen carefully to the murmur of 'atmos' (a sound engineer's term for the hum and whisper of background noise that we hear all the time). The very colours you see are your own feelings, drawn out onto and hitting the screen of experience. The tastes of things, the sounds of things, the play of straight lines and curves – in all these our own outpouring feelings flow into general meanings, gather associations, and so the world springs to life.[1]

This is the truth in the old Macrocosm/microcosm picture of the self and its world, as counterparts and as images of each other. On the one hand our outpouring feeling as it goes out into expression becomes clothed with general meanings, and our world takes shape and comes to life. At the same time we in turn are *ourselves parts of our own world*, so that the same process and current of feeling by which our world is enlivened and coloured is also the process by which *we ourselves* are also all the time coming to be and passing away.

The point of view I am trying to describe here is obviously both like and a little unlike that of Middle Way Buddhism, as classically set out by Nagarjuna. Buddhist practice perhaps aims to make the devotee equable, relaxed and even somewhat phlegmatic, and then Buddhist theory says that what is religiously liberating is the philosophical discovery that everything is Empty – insubstantial, flowing, interconnected process. Our unhappiness is diagnosed as fixated feeling, and is cured by the realization that there is no substantial being, either in the self or in the ambient world, for feeling to fixate upon. Very good, and I do not doubt that Nagarjuna's doctrine has worked and works as religion for people with relatively calm and equable temperaments. But if you are a Westerner and somewhat cyclothymic – that is, aware that the flow of feeling in you may vary in quality between mania and depression – then I think you may agree with me about the enormous religious importance to us of the outflowing river of life feeling in us, through which we live. It is capable of exalting each of us to Heaven, and of casting us down into Hell. The Buddha and Nagarjuna seem to be saying that by carefully following the Middle Way we can train the stream of life feeling in us into becoming so calm and equable that it can in effect be disregarded. Western asceticism (at first classical, and then subsequently Christian) sought to discipline the passions and to achieve self-mastery. I am arguing for a view slightly different from both of them, and more strongly life affirming. Each of us must seek, and religion should supply, the set of symbolic forms through which our world can become most richly beautiful and we can become most fully ourselves. And this emphasis upon our commitment to life, to the temporal flow of feeling, and to living by continually passing happily out into expression and away, is what I mean by 'solar' living. It is our redemption, understood in a fully committed and this worldly way. It is kingdom religion.

A Way of Living

Chapter Eight

H ere is a brutally sharp contrast: ecclesiastical religion was *believed*, but kingdom religion is simply *lived*.

Ecclesiastical religion was a state of waiting and readying yourself for a promised better world. It was highly reflective and credal: it was a matter of 'having faith', believing 'the Faith', and adhering faithfully to your Creed. Only God could actually bring in the better world, and the Creed was a supernatural story about how God had originally created the world and was presently at work redeeming it. Only the final denouement was still awaited, but it was very important that one should be vigilant in looking out for it – which in practice meant preparing for death. For most of the ecclesiastical period it was supposed that the basic conditions of human life here below could not be radically changed – as they needed to be – by anything less than the promised return of Christ. Religion was oddly pessimistic and passive: you valued correct belief, belief that *God* was changing things, so highly because there was so little that you could do yourself. Matters were largely out of our hands, as is shown by the striking fact that a 'Christian ethics', actively concerned for the betterment of society in the present age, scarcely developed *at all* before about 1770. As it developed it found itself to be chiefly if not entirely concerned with certain very specific humanitarian causes, and then in early Victorian times with the idealization of marriage and the family – with women and children, and with the worlds of domestic and private life. The Christianization of economic and political life, and of foreign relations, has in more recent times been more talked about than achieved. Thus although since the Enlightenment there has been a gradual turning of Christianity towards this world, progress has been slow and today it would still be fair to say that the practical side of ecclesiastical religion consists largely of 'observances'. Until 'in his own good time' God actually brings in the better world – or takes us to it – religion in the eyes of most people is going to remain an institution that is respected, a Faith that is to be believed, and a set of prescribed 'duties' that 'observant' believers fulfil. And that is it.

In summary, then, church religion is believed and 'observed', but people have seldom thought it possible to live it out in full. By contrast, Kingdom religion really is simply a way of living, which is popularly described as living life to the full, or to its fullest. In Church religion you very consciously are *not* one hundred per cent committed to life. No, because half of you is always a little detached, secretive, keeping your hands clean, thinking of eternity and preparing for death; whereas Kingdom religion is all-out solar, one hundred per cent, reckless. In its contemporary form it passionately loves what is living and only transient, *just for being transient.* Church religion is ulterior, long-termist and thinking ahead, whereas Kingdom religion is intensely focussed upon the Moment, the here and now, and is oblivious of everything else. It hasn't time even to *think* about cosmology: it lives at the end of the world. Church religion thinks and waits patiently. Kingdom religion *burns*: it is in a hurry because it understands that we are already in our last days. There is not much time left.

The contrast is extraordinary, and even more extraordinary is the co-existence of the two very different religions, side by side in the Sermon on the Mount and also in the wider tradition of Jesus' teaching. Sometimes Jesus is portrayed as urging his followers not to be anxious about the future but to live entirely in the present; yet at other times he is pictured as saying that you should be prudent and calculating, building your house upon a rock. Sometimes he says that believers should be solar, making an exhibition of themselves, as conspicuous as shining lights or hilltop towns; but at other times he says that all our religious duties, traditionally summed up as prayer, fasting and almsgiving, should be performed secretly. Sometimes Jesus talks Kingdom religion, as when he urges people not to hesitate nor to be self-concerned, but to plunge straight into moral action on behalf of others; but at other times he talks proto-Catholicism and says that our first concern should be for our own self-purification. We need to get the plank out of our own eyes before we can see clearly what's wrong with other people.[1]

In sum, 'the Sermon on the Mount' is a text strangely at odds with itself. Almost every verse either says *Think!*, like Church religion, or *Don't think!*, like Kingdom religion. The command *Think!* tells us to sort out our priorities, worry, reflect, recollect ourselves, cultivate self-awareness and plan ahead. The command *Don't think!* says that only the Now exists: live by the heart, trust life, plunge in, don't dither, give it all you've got, put on a good show, live as the Sun does. The contrast between the two character types and philosophies of existence is very great, so why are both outlooks attributed to Jesus – and why is the contradiction so rarely noticed?

The best answer we can give is that in the circles that preserved the tradition of Jesus' teaching people were already debating the issue between the two lifestyles. The 'Kingdom' people were more quakerish or existentialist in outlook: they wanted to continue to live in the Kingdom way and they 'heard' the sayings of Jesus as confirming their point of view. But the 'Church' party, closer to Paul, were conscious that the Kingdom had not yet fully come. In the waiting period it was necessary to come to some sort of accommodation with the old, violent social order and its institutions. People of this turn of mind, who urged reflection and calculation, also 'heard' the tradition of Jesus' sayings – but they heard it as confirming *their* point of view. So it came about that when all the sayings were collected and written down, they came to include both Kingdom sayings that said *Go the whole hog: be conspicuous*, and Church sayings that said *Work quietly and unobtrusively, like the yeast in the dough.* It is reasonable to suppose that Jesus himself had been an all out Kingdom person, with a very intense sense of eschatological urgency. He was ardent, vehement and disputatious, a man in a hurry. But after his death, how was his teaching to be preserved? Some people picked up on the 'Kingdom' sayings, and translated his eschatology into 'solarity', and other people picked up on the churchier sayings and translated his eschatology into 'inwardness'. What the world now calls The Sermon on the Mount (Matthew 5–7) reflects both points of view, so that when we read it we are not listening to Jesus, but overhearing a dispute amongst his followers.

To take the argument further now calls for a brief digression. The world of human life is tumultuous, excessive, unpredictable and many sided. Not even the very greatest of writers, not even Shakespeare can quite compass *all* of human life, and still less can any moral theorist systematize it satisfactorily. As a result, every moral theory and every body of moral teaching is likely to be found partial and incomplete. It prompts somebody to produce a counter theory or the contrary teaching, by way of protest or correction. An example of this that everyone has noticed is the way in which in popular morality over the generations the pendulum swings back and forth between rigorism and laxity, long skirts and short skirts, order and freedom, rule morality and welfare morality, longtermism and shorttermism, moralism and liberalism. When one of any of these pairs is pressed too hard, it is likely to trigger a reaction on behalf of its counterpart or 'Other'. And more generally, there is a case for saying that almost every moral theory and every important body of moral teaching functions as a *corrective*. Against what? – look at it in its original context. For example, Jesus' extreme emphasis upon religious immediacy, the imminent coming of the Kingdom of God, was expressly directed against an equally extreme form of religious mediation, namely the minute regulation of Jewish religious life by armies of scribes, lawyers, pharisees, sadducees, chief priests and the rest of them.

The dispute has often been repeated. In the Latin West the decline of the Roman Empire left something of a cultural and 'management' vacuum, which the Church filled. It took over almost the whole business of managing life, structuring time and space, teaching society's official world view, collecting a wide range of dues and inventing an even wider range of duties. An army of clerics/clerks found ways minutely to organize not just other people's lives, but even more, their own. If you doubt me, examine a Missal and Breviary and trace all the prayers that every Roman Catholic priest has been expected to recite every day. Similarly, the clerks found ways to bureaucratize the penitential system, prayers for the dead, and the efficacy of the Mass. There are always hapless souls who want life to be given 'meaning', and toiling away to win days off Purgatory certainly gives people something meaningful to do; but too much bureaucratization of religion was bound to trigger protest from a whole line of mystics and would-be Reformers. A surfeit of wearisome repetition eventually makes people quite desperate for religious immediacy. I know.

There is a further twist to this story: until the seventeenth century the great bureaucrats were clerics, and especially canon lawyers. But in the later seventeenth century we can see the last great 'ecclesiastical bureaucrats' – people like J.B. Colbert, finance minister to Louis XIV – beginning to turn into the pioneers of modern social administration. Great advances in the efficiency of filing systems were made in Napoleonic times, but it has been above all the computer which in very recent years has begun to make us the most minutely and efficiently supervised people who have ever lived. Life in the prosperous Western countries is becoming more closely and carefully structured, managed, regulated and optimized than ever before. It's becoming suffocating. We should not be surprised that people are not clamouring to have their lives *further* regulated, by the relatively archaic and inefficient religious systems that have come down to us from the past. On the contrary, in our time people prefer to engage in an independent religious quest: they seek religious freedom, personal experience, immediacy and even ecstasy. Religion is called upon to give us a break from our over regulated lives.

It is against this background that I argue that a reformed Christianity must now make the corrective move from discipline to freedom, from Church to Kingdom, and from 'organized religion' to pure religious immediacy. But we have no consolation to offer to those who seek to escape from this world into some 'spiritual' or supernatural 'realm' or 'dimension'. On the contrary, because of the way science, philosophy and modern culture have developed, the world of our life is now an outsideless continuum. There is nothing else but all this around us, of which we are integrally part. There is no distinct religious, or supernatural, or spiritual realm. Talk of other worlds or dimensions is empty. That is why our contemporary culture is rapidly becoming the most 'total' and all inclusive that there has ever been. Its only weakness is its secret terror of that which it cannot completely manage, namely the sheer contingency and transience of everything – and it is precisely *that* which Kingdom religion embraces most ardently. Kingdom religion attends to the gentle moment by moment pure givenness of all existence, the Be-ing of everything. It loves the meeting of Be-ing and language that makes the world of our experience so extraordinarily glowing and brightly lit in consciousness. It follows and it feels the *passing* of everything, recognizing that life is finite. Our love for life and our determination to make the most of it is tuned up and intensified by our knowledge that we have only so much of it left.

In a world in which it is easy to become numbed and bored by the way almost everything in sight has been made so safe and predictable, Kingdom religion restores freshness and urgency to living. We live *after* metaphysics, and there is no prospect of our being able either to escape from the world of life into another parallel 'spiritual' world or to find ontological depth and mystery within life. There is no depth. Nowadays everything is literally mundane. But we can greatly intensify our feeling for life by attending to just the features of life that most people don't want to think about, namely its very contingency, its temporality, and its finitude. Doing this can prompt us to love life and commit ourselves to it in its very transience. It is profoundly liberating to say Yes to life in its lightness and contingency, and to give up trying either to combat, or to forget about, the passing of time.

I think I now love the givenness and the contingency of everything more intensely than I used to love God. To love and accept life and death as a package is something altogether different from the more common state of clutching at life and being afraid of death. And I think that what I call Kingdom religion makes the merely human historical Jesus a bigger and more interesting figure than the old divine Christ. Jesus is the prophet who first taught people that one could live and love life with a fierce burning end of the world urgency. He frees us from church Christianity's curiously obsessive concern with cosmology – with describing and fitting us into a certain picture of the world order. We don't *want* cosmology: what we want is end of the world freedom.

To close this section and round off its thesis, I want to point out one respect in which Kingdom religion is like and another respect in which it is unlike Buddhism. They are alike in that both are logically independent of their own historical origins: they can be verified in practice simply by being lived. Church Christianity made itself vulnerable to historical refutation by pinning its own truth to certain very extravagant historical claims – in particular, about the resurrection of Christ. I think it clear by now that it was a mistake and is unnecessary to make your religion vulnerable in that way. Both Buddhism and Kingdom Christianity can be and must be verified in practice, just by being lived.

But here there is a difference. For Buddhism the great liberating truth is the truth of universal contingency. When we understand everything's lightness and contingency, we understand that there is no self-identical or substantial being. There is therefore nothing for 'craving' or 'fixation' to attach itself to – and we are free. Thus for Buddhism salvation is release from 'attachment'.

From the point of view of Kingdom religion Buddhism seems a little too unattached, cool and celibate. The Buddha is wise and compassionate: he does not experience suffering. Christ is furiously ardent: he loves and suffers greatly. Who do we choose to follow? It's up to you.

Chapter Nine

The Problem of
Self-Transcendence

Many or most church Christians who read this book will see it as proposing not the reformation of Christianity but the abolition of Christianity. This is because in its declining years church Christianity has become so very weak and self-centred. It has long forgotten the greater things for the sake of which it exists, and for the sake of which it should at the right time be happy to die. Yet it should not have forgotten these things, for they are still legible by anyone who looks out for them.

A simple example is credal belief. Church Christianity attaches the most enormous importance to correct credal belief. It is still instinctively felt both within the churches and outside them that a person who seriously impugns major items of belief should be swiftly and unceremoniously dumped. Yet at the same time it has always been known in the church that credal belief is only an imperfect and transitional state of mind. It promises to transcend itself, certainly after we die, and perhaps even in this life. When you have really worked through it, when your belief has become deep enough – then you no longer believe! Faith has given way to sight, and mediation to immediacy. Thus church Christianity actually works by progressively conducting us beyond itself, to a greater light on the far side of it.

The point was made with particular clarity in the Lutheran tradition, where Luther himself had taught that the believer should add a mental *pro me*, for me and on my behalf, after each clause of the Creed. Developing this idea, Kierkegaard speaks of the life of faith as 'an appropriation-process'.[1] All the doctrinal themes are meant gradually to sink in and become part of one's own being – which gives rise to the paradox that when you have fully become a Christian, you aren't one any longer. When you have internalized all the beliefs and have appropriated them into your life and practice, then you no longer hold them *as beliefs*, spelled out and with the brand names conspicuous. You don't *believe* it because you have *become* it and no longer need to spell it out.

There is, however, a problem: how can we tell that we have reached the post-missionary stage? When feminism, for example, as a missionary movement has fully made its point, and when its message is fully assimilated into everybody's life and practice, then it is no longer necessary – indeed, it has become inappropriate – to go on being an 'up front' or salient feminist, and the trademark jargon can be dropped. Have we reached that stage yet? It seems that we are betwixt and between, for on the one hand there are nowadays many women, especially in the West, whose acknowledged distinction is such that they do not *need* to be feminists. Their personal standing would if anything be compromised by an over salient profession of feminism on their part. But on the other hand there are also billions of women, especially in Africa, in Islam, and in South and East Asia, who still suffer very serious social disadvantage just because of their sex. So in the contemporary world feminism and post-feminism overlap: in most places salient missionary feminism remains the most appropriate posture, but in a few other places it is more fitting to ease off and be post-feminist. Feminism is after all meant to lead us beyond itself.

Then what about the case of Christianity? It is curiously complicated. In the West, Christianity evolved into radical humanism in the 1840s.[2] Since then the mainstream of Western culture has steadily moved over from 'Church' to 'Kingdom', with the gradual social establishment of liberal democracy, human rights, humanitarian ethics, the welfare state, environmentalism and modernism in the arts. This is a culture that in some ways has so fully assimilated Christian values that it no longer needs to be 'nominally' Christian – which is why it is currently dropping the old passwords and brand names. But religious conservatives are highly dissatisfied. They say that just as the state of Israel is a very unsatisfactory secular realization of Jewish religious hopes, so our comfortable Western consumerism and humanitarianism is a very unsatisfactory realization on earth of Christian eschatology. In reaction, conservative ultras both in Judaism and in Christianity therefore aggressively reassert the old supernaturalism and the old brand names. This is ironical: the Church exists for the sake of the Kingdom, but when the Kingdom comes the Church refuses to bow out gracefully, declares itself very disappointed, and fights back against the Kingdom! That is the very devil of a situation to sort out. But it's our present condition: several different ages overlap.

The same difficulty arises in relation to the Church. It knows perfectly well that it offers and teaches only mediated religion, and that mediated religion's only excuse for its own existence is that it is preparing us for the real thing, immediate religion, at some unspecified time in the future – perhaps at the return of Christ, or perhaps (and more likely) after we die. So we put up with the present state of discipline and with religious authority, for the sake of jam tomorrow. Then at the Reformation some groups thought that the time for the immediate, post-ecclesiastical 'Kingdom' type of religion had at last come. The Quakers, more recently called the Society of Friends, are the most notable surviving group from that period: they still retain an impressive and consistently worked out Kingdom theology, pattern of organization, and ethics. Through their very great contribution both to liberal democracy and to humanitarian ethics the Friends have been key figures in the making of the modern world. Ethically, the modern world is in many ways a Quaker world. Yet in Britain, where their spirit has been best preserved, they are now a tiny group, and the vast majority of Christians who remain are members of large episcopal Churches (Catholic, Anglican, Orthodox and a few others) which are structurally unable ever to make the transition from Church to Kingdom. The theology of episcopacy sees a diocesan bishop as being in his own person the Church in his diocese, so that a Council of all the bishops is an Ecumenical Council of the whole Church. Every bishop feels like the absolute monarch who said 'L'Etat, c'est moi'; and someone whose whole reason for existence is that he says to himself 'L'Eglise, c'est moi' can never allow the Church to pass over into the Kingdom, because he cannot possibly vote for his own abolition. He is locked into keeping the Church in being by promising jam tomorrow, forever.

Hence the paradox that in our own society the Friends have been showing since the later eighteenth century that kingdom religion is now possible and does work, whilst at the same time the vast majority of Christians remain permanently stuck in the age of the church – the modern Papacy being the most extreme example of the way mediated, institutional religion has forced itself up a cul-de-sac from which it cannot deliver itself. Having made an absolute of itself it cannot transcend itself, and therefore cannot actually function properly *as religion*.

I am saying that every episcopal church has a built-in and structural bias against ever allowing itself to pass over into the kingdom type of religion – for the sake of which it (notionally) exists! How did this paradoxical situation arise?

To answer this question we have to look at the period of the later Roman Empire during which the Church became the official state religion. Accepting establishment, the Church found itself locked into endorsing the existing social order, sanctifying it and proclaiming its benevolence and general satisfactoriness. That much is obvious: it's the merest cliché. But what is not usually noticed is the fact that as the faith of the Church became the official ideology of the Empire, so the Church became locked into a very strongly realistic and cosmological understanding of its own faith.

This intensely cosmological orientation of Church Christianity survives to this day. To this day the debate about 'science and religion', especially in the English-speaking world, focusses around attempts to weave together scientific theories about the origin of the Universe and of life, and theological doctrines about God's creation of the world, of life, and of the first human beings. Anglophone scientist-theologians have been arguing since Newton in favour of a condominium in which religious doctrine and scientific theory shall *jointly* provide the Establishment's world picture and combine to assure the common people of the wisdom and benevolence of the cosmic and social order. They passionately desire to ensure that physics, chemistry, biology and religion shall continue to coexist harmoniously in school and in university syllabuses, and that the Church shall continue to have a voice in the counsels of the nation — that is, in the Upper House of Parliament. They sincerely believe that a society in which the church is established is a Christian society. They want to sanctify the present world order, and they entirely forget that Christianity claims to be founded on a man who said that we should live as if we think that the present world order is going to pass away entirely very soon. Jesus wanted us to live *without* a cosmology, but we have got ourselves locked into equating true religion with living *on the basis* of a cosmology.

There is no doubt that the point here is curiously difficult for ecclesiastical Christians to grasp. So cosmologically minded have they become, so convinced are they that there is a readymade sacred cosmos, an objectively real and intelligible order of things out there which we are pre-designed to be able to understand and to live by, that they find it genuinely difficult to grasp anti-realist philosophy, and to grasp that there are major religious traditions which are *not* cosmological and do *not* regard the world as divinely created.

Nevertheless, the truth is that any reformation of Christianity *must* break the emotional and political link with cosmology. Kingdom religion is *post*-cosmological. You may perhaps only be able to learn this by having a really close brush with death, and learning how little the thought of the wisdom and benevolence of the established order of things means to you in that moment: but learn it you must. The totalizing notion of 'the Universe' may do a useful job in current physical theorizing, but it is of next to no religious or philosophical use. What has the Universe ever done for you? You should not try to found your own thinking on the idea of an immanent Logos that pervades the present world order, and you should not derive your moral values from the present world order. Our picture of the world order is only a human construct, and not a very satisfactory one. To think clearly in religion you should see everything as passing away, really passing away. You have to radicalize the idea of universal transience, as in their different ways Jesus and the Buddha teach you to do.

Put it another way: René Descartes founded modern critical thinking by requiring us to pass through a moment of universal *doubt*. He did not do this entirely consistently: indeed, he expressly excluded revealed religion and some other matters about which it was in those days not safe to urge doubt. But what he did say was enough to launch the project of modern critically tested empirical knowledge.

Then, two and a half centuries later, Friedrich Nietzsche radicalizes Descartes by requiring people who want to think clearly about questions of philosophy, ethics and religion to have looked *nihilism* in the face. This requirement makes Nietzsche still *the* modern philosopher, who clears our heads of the idea of substance and of the idea that something out there decides our values for us and tells us how we should live. He forces us to go back to the very beginning, and helps us grasp again the radicalism of Jesus and the Buddha.

Can church Christianity, seeking renewal and self-transcendence, really go back now to its own beginning by shedding all its structures and assumptions? It seems not. Yet it is true, as we noted earlier, that there are some 'Kingdom' elements within church Christianity. In particular, the Eucharist symbolizes the death of God and his distribution into the fellowship of believers; and Jesus expressly associates the Eucharist with the Kingdom. And secondly, Pentecost celebrates the empowering effect of God's ceasing to be Other and being instead poured out into human beings as Spirit. So both the Eucharist and Pentecost are *about* the coming of kingdom religion; and since they are both entrenched within the Church, might they not provide routes by which the Church could now seek to go beyond itself into the Kingdom?

Chapter
Ten

Is Reformation Possible? I

As was said earlier, we are talking about a reformation not just of the Church, but of Christianity itself. 'History' is understood as a preparatory or disciplinary stage in human development, during which people live under the rule of great institutions such as the State, the Church and the Academy. It has long been hoped that the disciplinary period would eventually come to an end, so that we humans may at last be able to live free of institutional domination. At the time of the Enlightenment various thinkers hoped that it was all beginning to happen. Human beings were coming of age, and the end of the old absolute monarchies and the rise of the new democratic republics was proof of it. Today similar hopes have been revived by the accelerating growth of knowledge, the spread of new information and telecommunications technologies, and cultural globalization. We begin to see what have been called 'the world religions' as having so far been in fact only local and rather narrow, locked into long obsolete ways of thinking. We begin to hope that Christianity may at last be able to outgrow the disciplinary 'church' form in which it has mostly lived hitherto, and move into its long awaited fully developed form.

The final and fully arrived incarnation of Christianity has been given many names: 'Jerusalem', the Kingdom of God on earth, the Kingdom of Christ, the messianic age, the sabbath rest of the saints and so on. At the Reformation in the sixteenth and seventeenth centuries the radicals wanted to go straight for it. As things turned out, Luther, the Princes and all the conservative reformers succeeded in putting a stop to that. They wanted church Christianity to continue, at least for the present and for the sake of civil order. Maybe they were right, but the radicals had put a whole range of new ideas into popular print, ideas that were to prove

65

unstoppable. In England there was a straight line of development from the Reformation to Europe's first democratic revolution, an event in which radical Christianity played an important part. It had put into circulation many of the key political and moral ideas of modernity: the idea of *freedom* – freedom of belief, conscience, expression, assembly and worship; the idea of *equality* ('the poorest he that is in England hath a life to live as hath the greatest he'); the idea of universal human enlightenment and liberation at the end of history – and so on. In short, since the Enlightenment the modern world has developed as in many ways a secular realization of the Christian hope. Universal education, internationalism, humanitarian ethics – do you see what it all means? It means that Christianity surely ought now to be able easily to step out of its decaying ecclesiastical vestments and into its new 'kingdom' form, because its new clothing is already out there waiting for it! To a considerable extent the new 'kingdom' form of Christianity already exists, for example in the great international humanitarian charities. In the coming years we may expect to see the Church peacefully declining and disappearing, and the spirit of Christianity passing over into the globalized eco-humanism of the future.

On this view the second Reformation, the passing over of Christianity into the global religious consciousness of the future, is already happening. We don't have to worry about it, nor to work at it. We need only to read the signs of the times and see it taking place. The veteran New Zealand theologian Lloyd Geering is perhaps the clearest and most explicit of those who interpret our present situation along such lines.[1] It does not really trouble Lloyd Geering that the church is ceasing to exist and its distinctive vocabulary is passing out of use. He is simply glad to welcome the new.

A different view is taken by John Shelby Spong, who recently retired as the Episcopal Bishop of Newark, New Jersey. He is, inevitably, an ecclesiastical Christian who addresses the church. He wants it to reform itself, beginning by urgently rethinking and revising its own doctrinal and moral convictions.

In this Bishop Spong stands in a long tradition of liberal protestant dissatisfaction with the cruelty and backwardness of Christianity as we have received it. Amongst such people during the nineteenth century Kantian teaching was very influential: they would invoke the Moral Argument for the existence of God, they tended to see Christian doctrine as a symbolic vehicle for moral values, and they were confident that Christian Ethics was and would remain the highest and noblest body of moral teaching known to humankind. Given this heavy emphasis upon ethical considerations, it is not at all surprising that the liberals should be very sensitive to the way political and social changes were beginning to make much of Christian doctrine seem morally cruel and out-of-date. Gods are moral postulates, and people tend to become like their gods. Do we really *want* to become like Calvin's God?

So when liberal Protestants think about the problem of reforming Christianity, they think first about a moral critique and purge of the system of Christian doctrine, such as had been carried out by Kant himself in his *Religion Within the Limits of Reason Alone* (1793). Their intellectual difficulties with traditional supernatural belief, when spelled out, are usually found to reflect discomfort with its *moral* implications. Like Socrates, the liberals see our religious duty largely in terms of living a good life; and (like Socrates, again) they think that we have a positive *duty* to correct morally unedifying pictures and stories about the gods.

For example, in an age when utilitarian social reformers were arguing for a remedial view of punishment, God's eternal retributive punishment of the wicked in Hell made liberals unhappy. In religious art, Hell has for millennia been depicted as a place of just the sort of 'cruel and unusual punishments' that the American Constitution forbids. How can we go on attributing to God cruelties that we have banned amongst human beings? Similarly, in a democratic age when people believe in checking and limiting power and quote Acton as maintaining that absolute power corrupts absolutely, liberals are bound to feel uneasy about the depiction of the Cosmos as the ultimate absolute monarchy, in which every deed and every event is foreordained, observed and judged by God. Furthermore, in an increasingly feminist age it is not surprising that people should begin to notice the extreme masculinism of the standard religious imagery that depicts God as an Almighty Father, the ultimate patriarch.

To turn next to the problem of evil, during the nineteenth and early twentieth centuries society was changing over, from an epoch in which the only recourse of the poor and needy was to pray for the occasional and gracious intervention of the rich and powerful, to a new age in which all needy citizens are legally entitled to benefits as of right. Unfortunately, God has always been depicted as operating in the *former* manner. When the needy cry out to him for deliverance he may occasionally intervene to heal and to feed, but he has not established under *all* of us a guaranteed safety net, a minimum standard of care for everyone, in the way that the welfare state has done. Why not? Why is God pictured as helping a few miraculously, but *not* as helping all routinely in the way that the state now does?

Liberal theologians, one may say, are people to whom the newer and more humanitarian moral values matter a great deal. They are very conscious that both in the Bible and in standard Christian doctrine harsh and very archaic moral attitudes are prominent alongside more congenial and loftier ideals. They feel unable to preach as gospel doctrines that owe more to Jehovah than to Jesus, and they want Christianity to repudiate and to purge itself of moral ideas that have become unbearable to decent people. And they appreciate that this will require a considerable doctrinal reformation. Their doctrine of God, for example, will tend to be very non-interventionist, and even to verge upon the 'non-realist' view that God is simply a guiding spiritual ideal, a moral postulate. God is not a causal agent, but a moral inspiration. God is . . . just *Love*, and Love is our God, and that's that – Johannine non-realism. In their account of the work of Christ, liberals tend to be exemplarists who see Christ's death as an acted parable of divine love, and they reject the sort of 'objective' theories that picture Christ as having placated God by bearing in our place the punishment for our sins. And in their account of human destiny liberals strongly favour the universalist view that in the end Hell will be empty, and all will be saved. But it must be acknowledged that liberal theologians in general give a very vague and shadowy account of life after death. Most of them wish to see Christian values prevail in this life, rather than wait until after death for their vindication.

In pushing this agenda the liberals have had some success – more success than you might suppose from their frequent complaints about the ferocity with which they are attacked by 'conservatives, evangelicals and fundamentalists'. It is true that the various conservative groups are numerically predominant within the Christian churches (as they also are in other religions such as Islam and Judaism); but the conservatives have themselves also been exposed to the same arguments and considerations that have weighed so heavily upon the liberals. If you enter a conservative religious milieu today, you will not hear any minister assuring proud parents that their new baby has been 'conceived and born in sin',[2] as orthodox doctrine asserts. One simply cannot say that sort of thing to people nowadays: they'd be outraged. And if you attend a funeral service in even the most conservative church, you will not hear an account of the Last Judgment that awaits every one of us, and an urgent call to repentance while there is still time. Nor will you hear any very detailed and specific account of either the pains of Hell or the joys of Heaven. Funerals, even conservative funerals, are no longer chiefly *about* repentance, nor are they even chiefly about life after death. For the fact is that very large areas of standard Christian doctrine have already been tacitly abandoned even by the most aggressively orthodox. The only difference between the conservatives and the liberals is that their more humane moral outlook constrains the liberals to be more honest about what has happened, whereas the conservatives prefer evasion and shibboleths because they will not openly admit that an older and harsher vision of the world has passed away, leaving a great deal of our traditional religious language virtually unusable. In order to gain a precious political advantage over the liberals, the conservatives claim to adhere to traditional doctrine in full; but the truth is that they *tacitly* modify traditional doctrine almost as much as the liberals do.

The conservatives cling to the old vocabulary, but cannot even begin to explain what it means. What *exactly* is 'God' supposed to be? How would you spell out to a friend with a decent scientific education just what happened when Christ 'rose from the dead'? If the Risen Christ rose bodily, and is still in his natural human body, then where is he now? Just what was it for him to 'ascend into heaven'? The conservative believer cannot *begin* to answer these questions. Hence the bewildering vacuity of Evangelical literature, in which words are used but nothing is said.[3]

Unfortunately, the liberal is not without problems of his own. Aware that with massive changes in our world view the old technical vocabulary of religion no longer has clear meaning, the liberal tries to translate it all into contemporary language. But the modern world being what it is, the words he is adopting do not already have established religious overtones and uses, and the completed translation inevitably fails to state a distinct position in clear language. Notoriously, liberals tend to find themselves accused of being woolly or vague. The old, cruel, hard edged vocabulary always seems clearer and more definite than the gentler vocabulary that the liberals are trying to put in place of it.

So much by way of background to what Bishop John S. Spong is trying to say in his recent publications, beginning with the book *Why Christianity Must Change or Die* (1998). He writes in the tradition of Paul Tillich and Bishop John A.T. Robinson, declaring that theism, 'the belief in an external, personal, supernatural and potentially invasive being' is no longer an option. Instead, to speak of God is to speak about the depths of our existence. In the Epilogue comes the positive statement, which begins:

> I believe that there is a transcending reality present in the very heart of life. I name that reality God.
> I believe that this reality has a bias towards life and wholeness and that its presence is experienced as that which calls us beyond all of our fearful and fragile human limits.

I believe that this reality can be found in all that is but that it reaches self-consciousness and the capability of being named, communed with and recognized only in human life.[4]

In the first and second paragraphs here, there are echoes of the language of Bonhoeffer and of Rudolf Bultmann. But exactly what Bishop Spong is saying remains hard to tell. He might be taken to mean that *life itself* is for him the religious object. I have tried to spell out elsewhere just what this might entail,[5] and my conclusion is that it is *not* what is being said here. Alternatively, Spong might possibly be understood as describing a metaphysical intuition of 'the Infinite in, with and under the finite', such as was described by the British philosophical theologian Austin Farrer: but I doubt it. He might be seen as teaching a version of my own non-realism: God is an ideal and an integrating concept that is *applied to* experience, rather than a reality that presents itself to us *in* experience. But Bishop Spong tells me (and I agree) that although we are in some ways close, he doesn't agree with my non-realism. Another possibility is that something of Martin Buber's personalism has reached Spong through John Robinson, but again I am unsure. Because he is a Bishop, Spong's language is required to be, and is taken to be, edifying and non-technical rather than philosophical. He has to use language which simultaneously suggests to some of his audience that he is making a radical break with tradition, and to others of his audience that the old realities remain reassuringly in place after all. These audience expectations exert an immensely strong pressure upon the speaker, to a degree that cannot be overemphasized. But the consequence is that someone who must speak and be heard mainly in a church context is not quite *allowed* to say anything too clear or definite. Perhaps for this reason, when he comes to write his *Twelve Theses* Bishop Spong says simply:

1. Theism, as a way of defining God, is dead. So most theological god-talk is today meaningless. A new way to speak of God must be found.[6]

It goes almost without saying that Bishop Spong is an interesting and courageous figure, whose work deserves to be treated with very great respect. But we see also that his case illustrates the familiar difficulties and the inevitable non-success of any attempt to initiate a new Reformation from a senior position within the Church. The political constraints upon his own use of language must make a Bishop sound vague, and as if what he is saying is designed to mean one thing to one section of his audience and another thing to another. He must speak as he does in order to get a hearing from the Church audience which is his constituency – an audience which is abnormally quick to take offence. It requires Church leaders always to give it 'a strong lead' – which means to reassure and flatter it, to fulfil all its expectations and defer to all its most irrational prejudices. If he ever says anything interesting and genuinely challenging to them, they will react with bewildered outrage, and his colleagues will instantly desert him (as happened with both John Robinson[7] and David Jenkins). If necessary they will publicly unite against him (as has happened with Bishop Spong himself). In a word, history has repeatedly shown at least since the Colenso affair in the 1860s that an 'honest bishop' cannot win. In the short term he may gain notoriety and goodish sales figures, but his long-term political failure is certain because of the way the group dynamics of the church operates.

Robert W. Funk is not so severely constrained by Church office as Bishop Spong has been. He can speak more plainly, and can be more philosophical. In the English-speaking countries, the combined influence of Calvinism and our native empiricism has made the general public remarkably literalistic in the way it 'receives' doctrinal statements (just as it is often similarly literalistic in its reception of works of art). If a bishop were to say plainly in public that doctrinal statements are not to be taken too 'literally' he would at once be understood to be saying that the doctrinal statements in question are just not true, and all hell would break loose. But Funk, as a theologian, is allowed to point out, for example, the special rhetorical character both of the Gospel narratives and Jesus' own utterances,[8] and he can then use this sort of observation as a base for opening a general argument about the nature of religious truth. In short, theologians have ways of being radical and getting away with it that are simply not open to bishops.

In his *Honest to Jesus* Funk remarks that 'When we use the term "God" nowadays, we find it necessary to put quotation marks around it to indicate how problematic the term has become'. In the revised *Twenty-One Theses* he is bolder – perhaps one might say, he is a Left Tillichian:

> 1. The God of the metaphysical age is dead. There is not a personal god out there external to human beings and the material world. We must reckon with a deep crisis in god talk and replace it with talk about whether the universe has meaning and whether human life has purpose.[9]

It is at once apparent that Funk can be and is more explicit than Spong. But he still runs into the same sort of difficulty. For what is being said in the last half sentence here? What *human beings* say and do may be meaningful and purposive, but there is no way of saying clearly that there are meaning and purpose out there, independent of us and ready-made for us. As Nietzsche sharply remarks: '*We* invented the concept "purpose": in reality purpose is *lacking*'.[10]

From this, I conclude that *on the negative side*, Spong and Funk are right, and obviously so. It is true that because of cultural and moral change, a good deal of standard Christian doctrine now has a bad smell morally. Living by it as it stands is actually *harmful* to people. It needs to be changed for the reasons that Socrates stated long ago: religious ideas are — amongst other things — moral postulates, symbolic vehicles for our values. Obviously we should not allow our lives to be guided and shaped by cruel and ugly religious ideas. We are quite right to watch out for the moral implications of our guiding myths, and to work at correcting them where correction is needed. On all this I warmly agree with Spong and Funk, to whom I am in many ways very close. But we need to understand the uncomfortable fact that liberal theologians have so far had little success in their project. They have taken archaic, rather ugly but undeniably potent traditional religious ideas and have tried to translate them into a more up-to-date and politically-correct vocabulary — but with what result? Alas, the modern translation almost always looks weak, and lacking in religious power. We may detest Augustine and Calvin, but we really cannot equal them. In the century since Adolf von Harnack published *The Essence of Christianity* (1900; Eng. Trans. 1901) we have had no success in creating a simpler and more morally acceptable version of Christian doctrine that is linguistically good and lively enough to push out and replace the weird old Western grand narrative theology left us by Augustine. It is true that theologians are allowed a little more freedom than church leaders are permitted, but there is no gain here. If a theologian such as Rudolf Bultmann writes well and does well, the response of the church is immediate: as has happened especially in recent years, the church simply erects a Chinese wall between itself and academic theology. The better we do, the more firmly the church will exclude us.

Why have we failed so badly in so important and even *easy* sounding a task? The best way to see the answer is to look at the state of religious language today in some other tradition: modern Islam perhaps, or India, or even a new religion such as Scientology. I fear that we are already in an epoch when any and every attempted spelling out of a system of religious doctrine sounds like nonsense. One struggles to read the texts, but finds that they are incomprehensible to an outsider. The insiders are people so desperate to feel that they belong to the group and so hungry for religion that they read these texts eagerly and believe that they understand them. They will seize upon and quote phrases as passwords, so as to create an illusion of comfortable familiarity and belonging. But it's all gobbledygook: and that is increasingly the position with *all* theological writing, whether Christian or not. It is *all* beginning to sound like the internal jargon of a cult, jargon intelligible only to insiders – and to them only for psychological reasons.

When we raise the question of reforming Christianity, people often suppose that this could be a simple matter. It could be done, they think, entirely within theology. All we need do is replace a lot of untrue and morally objectionable doctrines with a smaller set of true and morally edifying doctrines, and the job is done.

No: sorry. It is going to be *far* more difficult than that. Just to start with, we need to understand better why it is that *doctrine is dead* and the post-dogmatic kingdom type of religion is now the only live option.

Chapter Eleven

Is Reformation Possible? II

The liveliest and most interesting reformation proposals on the table today, such as those just discussed, by Spong and Funk, broadly follow the liberal protestant agenda classically laid down by Kant. A church leader or a theologian attempts a moral and intellectual critique of Christian faith and practice, cutting out the grosser elements of supernaturalism and the harsher pre-Enlightenment morality. When the Church's faith and morals have been thus simplified, liberalized and updated, then it will be easier for people of goodwill to remain her members.

There are one or two further points. For the last century or so it has been known beyond reasonable doubt that the only two great Christian dogmas that the undivided Church ever defined closely, namely the dogmas of the Incarnation and the Trinity, are wrong. Neither is fully scriptural. Of all the many New Testament theologies, only the Johannine teaches that in the Lord Jesus Christ a preexistent divine being has become incarnate amongst us, and *no* New Testament writer teaches the 'orthodox' doctrine of the full co-equal deity of Christ. But if the full doctrine of the Incarnation is unscriptural – and, what is more, is obviously incompatible with the fact that Jesus was a Jewish man who prayed to God, and cannot plausibly be pictured as having pretended to equality with the One to whom he prayed – if all that is so, then the dogma of the Trinity also falls.[1] And if the church has a policy of requiring men and women in training for the ministry to study theology, and if those people are learning from their studies that the most basic Christian doctrines can no longer be defended as being scriptural, or even as consistent with scripture, then the church, for the sake of everyone's mental health and its own long-term well-being, ought not to go on any longer requiring its officers to believe the unbelievable and defend the indefensible. Doctrinal revision is urgently necessary just on biblical critical grounds.

Conservatives and the powers that be in the church will of course reply that Christian truth has been revealed by God, and cannot be changed by 'man'. To which it must be replied that after 200 years' critical study of the history of doctrine it is surely now known beyond doubt that dogma has a history, and a very human history. People formulated and approved each item of orthodox doctrine, and some of the supporting arguments that looked good to them in the fourth and fifth centuries just don't look so good to us today. What earlier humans made, later humans may reappraise and redesign, or even discard. Certainly it is wrong to expect young people to study and to pass examinations in the history of Christian doctrine, and then to spend their whole lives preaching doctrine as if it fell from the sky ready-made and may never be rethought or even questioned.

To liberal theologians it seems absurd that the Church should needlessly handicap itself and damage its own members by clinging to irrational and morally objectionable ideas. They think that reformation by revising and updating the Church's teaching and practice is obviously both easy and necessary. So they put forward their proposals – and every time there is the same chorus of public indignation and outrage. In Britain, for example, there has been a storm over liberal theology every ten years or so since 1853. People never have time to attend to and learn from the arguments, but they do react instantly and very violently upon each occasion. Then it all dies down and is forgotten – until the next controversy comes along. Then once again it all comes to people as a bolt from the blue, even though the topic and the arguments – about the bodily Resurrection, the Virgin Birth, etc. – are almost unchanging. F.D. Maurice, *Essays and Reviews*, J.W. Colenso, *Lux Mundi, Foundations*, J.Y. Campbell's 'New Theology', J.M. Thompson, H.D.A. Major and the Modern Churchmen's Union, Hensley Henson's problems, Bishop Barnes, Bishop Robinson, Geoffrey Lampe, Bishop David Jenkins and Bishop Richard Holloway – these names were once all over the newspapers. Leader writers fulminated, correspondents prophesied utter ruin unless decisive action was taken against them – and now it's all forgotten, yet again. People have learnt nothing and remembered nothing. Liberal theology has made no progress and has achieved nothing. Unable to entrench any generally accepted results, it has never achieved take-off into sustained growth. In fact, critical theology generally has achieved nothing. In the two or three centuries of its life since John Locke and the deist controversies, critical theology has conveyed nothing to the public at large and has made almost no difference to the churches. Any member of the clergy who takes critical theology seriously in preaching will not prosper.

It seems then that the liberal reformation project has failed, and probably that it must fail. It fails partly for sociological reasons: religious bodies of every kind are controlled by religious professionals, who are mostly males and are therefore ambitious, competitive and hierarchically minded. The younger ones amongst them are actively competing for promotion and power, and amongst such people the moral high ground and political advantage will always seem to lie on the loyalist side, that is, the side of the established orthodoxy. So, although hopes of a liberal Pope have been aired in every election since the death of Gregory XVI, in our hearts we all know that a liberal Pope is an oxymoron, just as in England we all of us know that thought of any kind in a clergyman is a form of solitary vice. Thoughts are Doubts, and Doubts are temptations to be resisted.

But secondly and more seriously, since the early 1970s or so liberal theology has come to an end because it has been overtaken by the mighty cultural changes that have made it now impossible to utter any theological statements in the public realm that can be taken 'straight'. The old distinction between respectable and barmy religious language has disappeared, the distinction between a church and a cult has disappeared, and *all* doctrinal utterance has come to sound like the internal jargon of a sect.

The deep reason for all this is the end of metaphysical realism – the end of platonism, and the end of the appearance/reality distinction; the end therefore of the idea that the way things visibly appear to be is determined and is mediated to us by an invisible order, which may be called 'intelligible', 'noumenal', or 'spiritual'. None of us any longer actually thinks in terms of the old two worlds dualism which saw our life as being actively shaped all the time by an Invisible Reality behind the scenes. We are all of us in practice post-metaphysical nowadays: there are only the scenes, and they *have* no 'behind'. But almost all traditional religion, and certainly all of theistic religion, was like a picturesque platonism in the sense that it involved belief in the reality and the agency of gods, spirits, divine Grace, departed souls and other such invisible beings and forces. So the end of platonism is also the end of almost every traditional and otherworldly form of religious consciousness. And it is *a fortiori* the end of liberal theology, which was a middling plain person's attempt to make public rational and moral sense of something like traditional religious belief. Which explains why the surviving members of the last generation of prominent English liberal theologians all notoriously stopped having new ideas at some stage during the 1970s, and since then have largely disappeared from public notice. The journalistic bewilderment that greeted *The Myth of God Incarnate* in 1977[2] was a clear sign of the coming of an age that can no longer make any sense of religious thought. Indeed, people no longer see religion as a subject that can be profitably thought *about*.

Metaphysical realism, liberal theology and the public intelligibility of 'straight' theological statements all ceased in the 1970s then, at a moment which may be taken as the hinge between modernity and postmodernity. What have been the possibilities since that date? Amongst academics it is easy, as many distinguished examples testify, to avoid all controversy and become amazingly eminent simply by taking flight into history.[3] Others become unabashed and regret free post-Christians, along the lines that have been very well set out by Lloyd Geering.[4] There are many who hold such views in American Departments of Religion, but fewer as yet in Britain.

Those who want to go on publicly calling themselves Christians, and to offer some defence of their views, have a choice between refusing irony and accepting it.

(i) *The Evangelicals* refuse irony. Their method is to raise Anglo-Saxon anti-intellectualism to hitherto-undreamt-of heights. They refuse philosophy; they refuse critical theory, and they are untroubled by the fact that their language sounds like the internal jargon of a cult. They claim boldly that their internal jargon articulates real experiences that insiders genuinely have. It's all *true* – but in a way that only insiders can understand. So you must come over to us, if you want to verify our claims in your own experience. You need to be 'converted'.

(ii) *The Postmodernists* accept that the end of metaphysics has come upon us, and that it threatens us with nihilism. The *Right Postmodernists* who have flourished in Britain in recent years behave in a manner reminiscent of those undergraduates who enjoy playing up to the popular 'Oxbridge' myth. They are rather provocative neo-traditionalists. They simply *affirm* standard Latin theology, in a faintly camp, ironical and intellectually ungrounded manner. In this they may seem to resemble Barthians or partly Westernized Muslims, but I doubt if it is right to see them that way, for they are more consciously aestheticized than either of those groups. This – they are saying – is the myth we want to live by, and the game we want to play. These are the clothes we want to wear and the theatres we want to perform in. Our show has been playing longer and our story reaches more people than any other show in town. In fact, it's our story, it's the *best* story, and we are sticking to it. On such a basis many of the younger members of the clergy, especially in the biggest cities, can easily pass for being impeccably 'orthodox'. Some of them honestly think they really *are* orthodox, a thought that gives me a headache.

The alternative view is that of the Left Postmodernists, who seem to combine the Right Postmodernist diagnosis of contemporary philosophy and culture as being nihilistic with elements of very old-fashioned liberal seriousness. Left Postmodernists accept the metaphysical 'truth' of nihilism, and therefore accept that the meaning of theological statements cannot be understood realistically. But this opens the way for a regulative understanding of the way religious ideas work: they show us how *we* can and must build, value, and revalue our world, and so conquer nihilism by the way we speak. We are *supposed* to play God, for God's sake! Left Postmodernists admire Buddhism, and see nihilism as being in some ways a profoundly liberating doctrine. But whereas Buddhists praise pure contingency and cling to the Void, left-postmodernist Christians are religious humanists who cling rather to the empty flux of 'life', the passions and the human world. Most recently, they have come to think of themselves as post-ecclesiastical Kingdom Christians (because of course 'they' are, roughly, me – and a few others).

Such are the options for serious religious belief now. You can be an unironical Evangelical, whose religion works like a cult because it is verified by experiences that are vouchsafed only to insiders. You can be an ironical Conservative, or 'Right-Postmodernist', who is ironically aware of but content to live with the distance between the world of her religion and the world of our secular postmodernity. In defiant mood, the Right Postmodernist affirms the Gospel vociferously: 'This is my Story, and I'm stuck with it'. And finally you may be a Left Postmodernist, who gives up all doctrinal claims and stops trying either to defend or to reform the Church. Neither policy is feasible now. Instead, the Left Postmodernist diagnoses our contemporary Western culture, with its humanitarianism-in-the-Void and its conceptual art, as an (imperfect) secular realization of the Kingdom of God. He doesn't try to beat it: *he joins it,* and seeks to make a religious contribution to its development. He wants it to become aware of its own religious origins and possibilities.

In this present book we are proposing and defending the Left Postmodernist strategy. We do not propose church reform, holding it to be impossible for two reasons: the first is that the internal power structure and the group dynamics of the Church combine to ensure that the

Church will always successfully resist reform to the bitter end. In the early sixteenth century, the cause of reform was able to gather momentum only because various princes in Northern Europe quickly took Luther's side, seeing in church reform an opportunity to make a very significant political gain for themselves. Today that external political backing for reform is simply not going to be forthcoming and the Church, even in its own death throes, will easily see off all would-be reformers. And the second reason why there cannot be a liberal reformation is that the intellectual breakdown of theology has now gone so far that there is no prospect of liberal theology being once again able to set out an intellectually respectable core syllabus of religious belief. *On strictly rational grounds*, you have no reason whatever to be pleased that your daughter has become a nun rather than a Moonie – and everybody knows it.

The present situation in Christianity may usefully be compared with the situation in Judaism, where secular Zionism achieved its goal in 1948, and many saw in the founding of the state of Israel a secular realization of the old religious hope for a Restoration of Israel. The crucial theological issue is this: can one be *religiously content* with a fulfilment of one's religious hopes that has come about, not by a special intervention of God as one had hoped, but merely by the ordinary course of historical events? The ultra-Orthodox (nowadays, Gush Enumim and the Shas) are *not* content. They refuse to recognize the religious legitimacy of the state of Israel, and may occupy themselves with minor acts of sabotage such as obstructing building development – usually on the grounds that there are Jewish bones in the soil on the site. The Shas, like 'fundamentalists' everywhere and in all religious traditions, refuse to see religious value in secular culture and attempt an aggressive reassertion of the most specifically and narrowly religious values. But the great majority of Israelis have little time for the Shas. Secular Israelis love their Jewish heritage (in a non-realist way, of course), but they also like the Enlightenment values – democracy, human rights, pluralism and all the transient joys of life. 'Why *shouldn't* we see in modern Israel a secular fulfilment of the old faith? If the Shas were to take over, what kind of society would *they* create?' Going further, a 'Left Postmodernist' Israeli could argue: 'Our contemporary world is *already* a much better world than the one the ultra-Orthodox would like to take us back to; but in order to get rid of them and their protest we need to go further. We must invent kingdom Jewishness: we must invent new Jewish values and lifestyles, appropriate to our own historical epoch. We have to make religion that is better *as religion* than the religion of the ultras. When we have done so, we will have removed their reason for existing.'

The situation in Christianity is analogous, but on a very much larger scale. Since around the time of the First World War the old hierarchical and disciplinary culture of the West has been steadily replaced by a new and very populist culture of leisure and self-expression. Its politics is liberal democratic, its world view is humanitarianism-in-the-Void and conceptual art, its spirituality is a solar affirmation of life, and so on. Historically, this new culture is rooted in radical Christianity and in European history, but its twentieth-century efflorescence owes much to the USA, which has for nearly a century been the world's leading country. The reason for this American preeminence is that from its beginnings America has at its best been a dream of pure religious freedom and an attempt to build the Kingdom of God on earth. Do we understand that the most religiously new and noble thing about America is its *secular* tradition?

I have argued that we should recognize in this new and increasingly globalized Western culture a secular fulfilment of the Christian hope. If we can show this new culture its own history and its own religious significance, and if within it we can pioneer new religious values and lifestyles, then we will indeed gradually 'build Jerusalem' and turn it all into as full a realization of religious hope as there can be.

One major obstacle to this project is the Christian version of the Shas – the army of pessimistic religious conservatives amongst us who simply hate the new culture and see it as being nihilistic and as the product of a great rebellion against God. I think they are wrong. They do not know their Bibles well, and have largely forgotten their kingdom theology. Two hundred years ago thinkers like Kant and Hegel still understood how it is that in the transition from ecclesiastical theology to kingdom theology 'theological realism' is left behind, God ceases to be a distinct being and moves into immanence. There is no separate religious realm, no Temple in Heaven; and mystics know that in the Unitive State one does not experience God as a distinct Being. But my own experience has suggested that the decline of theology has now gone so far that neither church leaders, nor theologians, nor even philosophers of religion any longer understand kingdom theology. This lack of understanding leaves them stuck in ecclesiastical theology, and unable to use it as a ladder up which to climb beyond it. So, like the Shas in Israel, they cannot see religious value in today's seemingly secular realization of traditional religious hopes.[5]

An amusing illustration of the interplay of ecclesiastical and kingdom thinking, which may illuminate the issues here, is the case of marriage. Although it developed late, 'Christian marriage' is one of the more attractive and durable creations of ecclesiastical religion. It seeks to moralize nature. It is long-termist and disciplinary. By reciprocal life vows something unconditional is fixed in the temporal world. Fine: but in kingdom religion marriage ceases. Its jealous, exclusive and disciplinary character marks it as belonging to the 'historical' age of the Church, and when the kingdom comes there is to be no more marrying and giving in marriage.[6] As radical Christianity has always known, the kingdom period is an age of Free Love. And today, it's all happening: the old patriarchal structures are melting away and marriage has come to seem unnecessary. Marriage is dying out – one more sign that the kingdom epoch has begun. We are learning to use sex as being simply the best and richest form of interpersonal exchange. It was at this point that an alarmingly intelligent friend objected to me: 'Then why are *you* so uxorious? Marriage is pure ecclesiasticism. If you really want to move on to the kingdom era, you should start practising Free Love *now*'.

If you have kept up with the argument, you should be able to guess my best reply: In the kingdom, one possible form of Free Love is that which decides to keep choosing and winning the same partner afresh each day. That is 'solar' marriage, right? We forget the former longtermist, disciplinary, jealous and exclusive character of marriage, and go instead for solar marriage-in-the-Void, or marriage 'till death'.

An equally amusing contrary example is this: the Lesbigays are highly 'Kingdom', so why are they trying so hard to win full acceptance in the Church? Cupitt is morally Church, but trying to pass himself off as kingdom; and the Lesbigays are morally Kingdom, but trying to get into the Church. Why are these people so keen to be amphibians?

The answer to this question gives the answer to the question of reformation. It is as follows: conceptual art still needs a traditional art gallery to provide it with the setting in which its meaning *as art* can be recognized; and similarly, emergent kingdom religion needs a church background to provide it with the setting in which its innovative religious significance can be read most clearly.

Chapter Twelve

Framing Reformation

Until about the mid-twentieth century works of art were usually framed. A sculpture rested upon a plinth or, if it was an indoor piece, on a small stand. A painting was surrounded by a gilt frame that distinguished and separated it from its surroundings, so that looking at it was like looking through a window at an outdoor scene, or through a hatch in an interior wall at an indoor scene. The frame said: 'Look at this!'.

Then the subject matter and also the styles of works of art began to diversify greatly, and many artists discarded the frame. They wanted to warn the viewer that what they were doing was something rather new, and they wanted it to stand alone, with nothing to direct us to look at it in one way rather than another. In art galleries, paintings had come to be arranged in national schools and in historical sequence, but modern painting wanted to break with history and nationality. If the public complained that it was becoming difficult to tell what was intended to be viewed as art from what was not, the answer was that art is stuff that has been made by people recognized as artists, and is sold by art dealers, and displayed in art galleries. Its institutional setting shows you that it is still art, even though it is different from what art has been hitherto.

Since the artists don't want us to have too many preconceptions, there has been a desire to make the setting in which art is displayed as cool and neutral as possible. The Saatchi Gallery, in Boundary Road, St John's Wood, London is a good example. It was created out of a group of large disused industrial workshops which are windowless and lit only by glazed rooflights. Inside the architect has created smooth, white and unadorned walls and floors, so that visitors seem to be drifting about in a great white void. The gallery has been made into as minimalist and neu-

tral a space as possible for the display of the kind of art that Charles
Saatchi likes – aggressively unhistorical, ungenteel, unaesthetic, in-your-
face and up-to-the-minute. I like it: but even in its very minimalism the
Saatchi Gallery is still busy interpreting the work that it displays. Everybody knows that Saatchi is an advertising man, trained to fasten upon
whatever is as eye-catching and up-to-date as possible, and by making his
Gallery a Nowhere place he warns us to expect to see in it works that
come from Nowhere and sock us in the eye. If we go to the Saatchi
Gallery we are asking for it, and we duly get it.

In short, Saatchi's Gallery is the ideal place in which to view the
kind of art Charles Saatchi likes and buys. He has, as they say, 'made' a
whole generation of artists. Important patrons of art do that: their taste is
interpretative. For whatever people say to the contrary, a frame is always
needed, and is always provided. Taking the argument a stage further, the
philosopher Arthur C. Danto adds that a work of art is always born into
an 'artworld' – a circle of people, an historical context, and an ongoing
process of critical reception and assessment.[1] The work of art historians
and art critics also 'frames' art and gives us vocabulary in which to discuss
what we see.

In summary, the lesson of this illustration is that even the most anti-
historical and innovative artwork is socially 'made' or constituted as art
by the patron whose taste picks it out, the setting in which it is displayed,
and the context of institutions, history and criticism which receives it. All
this material 'frames' the work and attributes 'meaning' to it; and all art
needs to have such an interpretative frame and social embodiment.

Now to apply this analogy to our present questions of a new reformation of religion. Where is it to occur, how is it to be recognized, and
what 'frames' it and interprets it?

The question is curiously interesting and difficult. We've been talking about whether what remains of the Church may perhaps one day be
prompted to reform itself, either by one of its own leaders, or by the writings of a theologian. We have decided that it is very unlikely to happen,
because all religious bodies are highly protective of their own traditions
– and become even more so when they feel threatened. New ideas are by
definition *wrong*, and least of all can the Church accept the notion that
the epoch of mediated, creed based, church type religion is now over and
it is time for us to move on to the final stage of Christianity's historical
development, the 'solar', immediate kind of religion that was traditionally called 'the Kingdom of God'. The sixteenth-century reformation went
only halfway, and stopped at being a reformation just of the Church. This

time there is no alternative but to go straight for the kingdom; and I have for some years past been attempting to show what kingdom religion will be like. Kingdom religion is humanism-in-the-Void, it is post-historical and short-termist, it is expressive, 'solar' living, and it is an intensely religious love of life. If you like to use traditional language and to cite authoritative texts, as I do in this book, it is the religion of the Sermon on the Mount. 'Ecstatic immanence', perhaps.[2]

The relation between ecclesiastical religion and kingdom religion is analogous to that between the traditional realism in painting and the expressionism that came in increasingly from the 1880s, as the Modern movement got under way. For the old realist outlook there had been an objective order out there — whether of supernatural realities, or of Nature — and the painter copied or represented it. One *received* truth: one took it in and copied it down faithfully. But in the new expressionist outlook everything is turned the other way round. In art and in life, the self pours itself out into expression. In its self-expression it continually becomes itself and passes away, living a dying life. And by the very same process our world is continually formed and coloured up. Hence the phrase 'humanism-in-the-Void'. Kingdom Christianity is like Buddhism qualified by Jesus' eschatological or 'solar' urgency and love of life. It is the *telos*, the End of all things. But how is it to be framed and recognized? What kind of social embodiment can it have? It is so intense and immediate that most people cannot see it as religion, so what is going to interpret it to the public?

My answer is that the Church is still the necessary theatre; partly because the church is still the best public space or theatre in which to proclaim and test out new initiatives in lifestyle and spirituality; and partly because the church, despite itself, still carries deeply buried in its memory the necessary concepts for explaining and interpreting Kingdom religion. That the church is still the best available frame and theatre is recognized by all those people who use it and borrow its vocabulary in order to propagate their Liberation theology, feminist theology, black theology, green theology, black feminist theology, and so on. Lesbigays do not scruple to use the church — or what is left of it — as a useful theatre and proving ground in which to pursue the cause of the social emancipation of sexual minorities: and I think they are right. After all, the various causes named — the emancipation of the poor, of women, of minority races, of sexual minorities, and of the earth itself — these are all good solid kingdom causes. So why should we also not take encouragement from them, and pursue the ultimate unscrupulousness of using the church as an arena in which to attempt to try out and propagate even *Christianity?* It sounds a splendidly cynical strategy, but the church does still provide the right and necessary contrasting backdrop. Notice, though, that the project we are talking about here is not the same as Kierkegaard's project of attempting to smuggle Christianity into Christendom. He meant, trying to smuggle what *he* understood to be real Christianity into an indolent, self-satisfied, middle-class culture that fancied itself Christian. But his conception of 'real Christianity' was traditionally strenuous and ascetical, and his attitude to the Bible was largely pre-critical until he read D.F. Strauss towards the end of his sadly abbreviated literary career. He never fully grasped the depth of the chasm between 'the Jesus of history and the Christ of faith' – a phrase introduced only in 1865,[3] many years after Kierkegaard's death –and he never properly developed the contrast between ecclesiastical religion and kingdom religion. The most you can say is that whereas the early 'aesthetic literature' praises a religion of hidden inwardness, the 'second literature' calls for more self-outing. A generation or so later, Vincent van Gogh undergoes a similar development from the earnest young evangelist to the superlatively passionate, solar kingdom religion of his mature painting. Evidently the contrast between ecclesiastical religion and kingdom religion was only very gradually becoming clearer during the nineteenth century. Today it is or should be clear to everyone who has studied the Bible at university level.

The church – or what is left of it – provides kingdom religion with a good frame because of its own complex, ambivalent relation to it. The Bible and church history – especially the history of mysticism, and the history of the radical wing of the Reformation – supply a broad categorization of kingdom religion, and also supply the idea that the church is a transitional disciplinary institution that was meant to be preparing us for the freedom of the Kingdom: but the vehemence with which the church can be relied upon invariably to *reject* the Kingdom makes very clear the ironical, dialectical relationship between the two. Thus the church says piously, 'Now we see in a glass darkly, but then face to face': but when people dare to come along and *practise* immediate, beliefless religion, the church immediately rises up in anger and expels them as *unbelievers* – because the church has entirely forgotten that 'belief' is not an end in itself, but is only for the sake of a post-credal *immediate* relation to the religious object to which we hope to proceed as soon as we can. In fact, just about *everything* in the church is a means of some kind which has been fetishized and turned into an end in itself – a point which can be demonstrated clearly by any attempt to live and practise kingdom religion within the church.

An amusing example, worth theological study, is given by the history of the relationship between the painter Stanley Spencer, an instinctive kingdom Christian, and the Church and people of the village of Cookham-on-Thames, Berkshire, England during the years 1918–1957 or so. During his painting career Spencer imagined the Gospel events taking place in the village. Many of his works were painted with a view to their hanging in the parish church, or in an enlarged and idealized version of it. But he was regarded as a scandalous figure, whom most villagers avoided. Two people known to me, who were young girls in Cookham in the early 1920s, were taught that when they walked down the road where Spencer lived they must cross to the opposite pavement in order not to pass dangerously close to his house. At one time Spencer was even threatened with prosecution for obscenity by the then President of the Royal Academy (Munnings). Only at the end of his life, with his knighthood, could he be granted a measure of acceptance and a retrospective exhibition in the parish church. Since his death his reputation has grown steadily, and his work today commands higher prices at auction than that of any other British artist since Turner. In retrospect, Cookham is now actually proud of him. And perhaps the 'kingdom' sort of Christianity may similarly become intelligible and even acceptable in retrospect.

Throwing Off
the Painted Veil

A long tradition, derived ultimately from Plato, describes the whole world of sense experience as 'a painted veil' that hangs between us and the eternal world.[1] I'd like to borrow that metaphor: the whole picturesque world of mediated religion – doctrine, scriptures, organization, the Calendar, rituals, art – all hangs like a painted veil or an iconostasis between us and something we are very afraid of, something we haven't yet confronted, to which the only fitting response is the practice of immediate religion. Mediated religion is very self-absorbed, and much of its energy is devoted to propagating and explaining itself. Thus nearly all of preaching is devoted to explaining scripture, explaining Christian doctrine, explaining the Church's various rituals, explaining the symbolic significance of the current season, or the Feast now being celebrated, and so on. The painted veil loves to elaborate and enrich itself; indeed, it tends to become an end in itself. We have tended to use it as a shield, to protect ourselves from whatever lies on the far side of it. We love it for making the unknown bearable. Now, however, the shield does not work any more. We are talking about reformation, and about throwing off the entire painted veil. That means that in the next Reformation the destruction of symbolic material will have to be on a very much larger scale than last time.

I say, *very* much larger. Imagine that you are watching Salome performing her erotic dance, and casting off her seven veils one by one – until the last veil is discarded, leaving *nothing at all*, and one realizes that her physical presence and her allure were only an illusion created by the movement of the veils. All men have moods in which they darkly suspect that the magnetic attractiveness to them of women is a magical illusion created by social conditioning, by manner and gesture, by jewellery, cosmetics and grooming, by peekaboo tricks of revelation and concealment, and so on. But, these same men mostly decide, it is an illusion from which they do not in the least want to be freed. They do not want the naked truth, because it is a no-thing. They prefer to cling to the painted veil.

So it is with religion. In order to move forward from Church religion to kingdom religion we must be ready to throw off the entire painted veil, giving up all the doctrine, giving up all the brand names, and giving up the whole magical illusion of mediated religion. Your average Church person whose whole life has been given to the painted veil already knows in her heart what will remain when it is all thrown off – nothing. That is of course the deep reason why the Church today does not *want* reformation, and doesn't *want* to cast off the painted veil. It claims to be realistic in its faith: that is, the Church claims to believe that the painted veil is a true picture; that is, it claims to believe that the images on the painted veil add up almost to a colour photograph of the eternal world and its inhabitants. The symbol somehow *copies* the divine reality that it symbolizes. So the Church claims to believe, and woe betide anyone who dares to question the claim. But amongst conservative religious apologists dogmatism and scepticism have for centuries been very closely intertwined, with each masking the other and each pretending to be the other's only alternative. Thus since early times dogmatic platonists, orthodox Jews, Catholics, Muslims and Reformed or Evangelical protestants have all been wont to claim that anyone who questions their dogmatism is in danger of dropping straight into the final damnation of scepticism or nihilism; whilst in the same culture areas sceptics have believed themselves to be trapped in infinite regresses and vortices of doubt from which they can be rescued only by finding and clinging to a dogmatic rock. The only alternative to dogma is scepticism, and the only way out of scepticism is by accepting dogma. Thus it is that so-called 'conservative' religious believers are nearly always either dogmatists who harbour a secret terror of scepticism, or natural sceptics who have clutched at the nearest available dogmatic lifeline: and it is these very people who become idolators, that is, fundamentalists who cling to the painted veil of mediated religion as if it were *itself* the only thing that can save them. They are fanatical dogmatists who can't bear to face the truth that they know in their hearts, namely that behind the painted veil there is only what is variously called universal contingency, universal Emptiness, Nothing and 'Being' – or what I might prefer to call Life's awesome pure contingency, givenness, transience, sweetness and nihility.

I will tell you the truth about the conservative believer – a truth which I think has never been told before. As he approaches death he comforts himself with the thought that he will never know he was wrong, and will never have to face the falsification of his faith. So he dies full of hope for the afterlife – and that is the end of him. Personally, I am sorry for him, because he never lived. He never fully acknowledged the truth of life, and never knew the supreme religious joy of solar living. He wanted only to die full of faith and in a state of grace. So he stuck rigidly to the painted veil of ecclesiastical religion, and did all that it required of him. He believed it all, that is, he never allowed himself seriously to doubt that he believed it all. But there remained a vital corner of himself that took secret comfort from the thought that, in any case, if I die in the odour of sanctity *I'll never know that I was wrong, and nor will the survivors who honour my memory ever really be certain that I was wrong.* So I win, because I shall never be fully and finally exposed as having been wrong.[2] Future generations will envy me my faith: such is the unexpected way in which on my deathbed my scepticism comforts my dogmatism.

On that very quiet pact between dogmatism and scepticism ecclesiastical religion has rested at least since the end of the Middle Ages. Many, many people feel – or have felt until very recently – that the argument is persuasive. Don't we envy those who died happy in faith, and never knew that they were wrong? Don't we envy the Egyptian Pharaoh, sealed for eternity in a gilded cocoon of royal ideology that unites him with Osiris?

The test is this: suppose that you are at the bedside of the dying Pope. Would it be ethically right to try to disillusion him, or should you take the view that it is better to let someone die happy, in error? Until as recently as the early 1990s I remained reluctant to disturb the illusions of the dying, but the influence of Brian Moore's novel *No Other Life*[3] has worked on my imagination for seven years, and anyway, I'm getting old myself now. Since the mid-90s I have thought that after Nietzsche we human beings no longer have any excuse for lying to ourselves. In our hearts we more than half know the truth about our life. Until we have looked it full in the face we haven't yet become adults, and until we have tried solar living (which is newspeak for what used to be called 'eternal life') – until we have tasted solar living we simply haven't known what religious joy in life can be. Even on one's deathbed it's not too late to become what a human being should be. If we miss out in this life, we miss out forever, because there is no other life. And this is so important that it should be said even to a dying Pope. It is so important that it is even worth trying to persuade Christians to try to reform their own faith, by casting off the painted veil and giving themselves a mortal fright at the sight of what lies behind it, and so working their way painfully towards kingdom religion. And why *shouldn't* one commit the ultimate, impossible heresy of trying to persuade Christians to start taking Jesus seriously?

Chapter Fourteen

Solarity and History

Why is it so hard to imagine the church ever being persuaded to take Jesus seriously? Two main reasons are given. The first is that the Western Church gradually developed into the largest and grandest system of mediated religion and pyramid of spiritual power that the world has ever seen. But Jesus was above all else a critic of just this kind of religion. Therefore it cannot take him seriously. And the second reason is that Jesus' solarity – his intensely *focussed* form of consciousness – is typical of a prophet or visionary whose thought jumps straight to the End of All Things. He has no time for relativities and means, no time for the long haul of history or for any large scale social thinking; and that is why people who have big responsibilities can have no time for him. He was in too much of a hurry, and perhaps he had to be: but our problems are different from his. We have to think in centuries.

These two issues – Jesus' relation to mediated (or 'institutional', or 'organized') religion and the relation of his outlook to history – need to be discussed if we are to make progress.

The main burden of Jesus' criticism of both synagogue and Temple is clear enough. It shows in the sheer number and variety of his opponents – 'chief priests, scribes, Pharisees, Herodians and Sadducees'. As the apparatus of mediated religion grows ever more elaborate, so whole classes of people arise who have a heavy personal investment in it. They are so attached to its rituals and its privileges that they cannot and will not recognize the hour of its fulfilment – or alternatively, the decisive Moment at which one should break clear of it. It is as if you have made such a ritual out of praying for the coming of the Kingdom that you'll never be able to see and seize the Moment of the Kingdom's coming. In the synagogue the old men with their prayer shawls and phylacteries and their reserved seats nod their heads piously as the long familiar prophetic texts are read yet again. They are so set in their ways that when Jesus heals in the synagogue,[1] and when he gets up and says, 'Look! It's all beginning to happen! This is what you've been waiting for!' – then he starts a riot and they want to kill him.[2] Their vigilant waiting for the Kingdom has become a ritual that they will not give up; no, not even for the Kingdom itself.

In the Temple the message is the same, but still more so, for the Temple is a classic example of a system of religious mediation that has grown so big that it consumes almost the whole of a people's agricultural surplus. It is like the Church in the Middle Ages: it still prays 'Thy Kingdom come', but the clergy are so numerous and they are doing so *well* that they are all of them in effect adding sotto voce '– but not in my time, please; not just yet'.

The Temple is mediation, instrumentality, the long view and 'all in due order' (Latin: *rite*). The Temple is a mighty social institution, convinced of its own social importance and proud that it 'thinks in centuries'. Jesus pits against it his own eschatological, or 'solar', kind of consciousness. This relatively novel kind of consciousness is very intense, immediate and short-termist. It focusses one's eye on the ball so closely that one thinks of nothing else at all. It scorns all long-term planning and instrumental thinking, to such an extent that all value becomes intrinsic. In Jesus' outlook everything tends to become either infinitely important, or a complete waste of time. Value must be recognized, seized, enacted, affirmed just *Now* and at this Moment. (Notice that whereas Eckhart's *Nu*, his Now-Moment is more mystical, Jesus' Now-Moment is more moral. You seize it, not by being receptive to it, but by deciding for it and committing yourself wholeheartedly to it.)

Now the crucial point: most people who think about the contrast between extreme long-termist and extreme short-termist styles of thinking assume that the long-termist kind of thinking is the more 'historical'. That is, it seems at first sight obvious that the Temple's long-termist kind of religion is more historically minded than the extreme urgency and short-termism of a prophet like Jesus. Along such lines established church type Christianity likes to declare, in a self-congratulatory tone of voice, that 'Christianity is an historical religion' – meaning that it is a large and socially entrenched system of religious mediation that attaches great importance to its own remote historical origins, to tradition, to degrees of sacred rank, and to the punctilious performance of an annual cycle of grand rituals. Such a system takes many centuries to evolve and lasts for millennia. It looks back over a very long past, and forward to an equally long future. It is *very* historically minded; whereas those shabby ranters, preaching in the open air to gawping crowds . . . pooh! People, I am suggesting who are involved in large-scale 'organized religion' are apt to see themselves as important persons who have a strong sense of history, and they are apt to see Jesus as having been profoundly *anti*-historical. He was an over-excited prophet of the End of History who turned out to be simply mistaken. We need to recognize, they say graciously, that his foreshortened perspective did enable him to see some things – 'ultimate' things – more clearly than the rest of us, but on the main point he soon turned out to have been mistaken. Elijah did not appear to take him down from the Cross. He died, history has continued, and here we are.

So it is said: but I want to reverse it, and to argue instead that it is not the religion of Jesus but the religion of the Temple that is really anti-historical. The Temple takes people *out* of history and into the dreamtime of a great myth that is recycled liturgically year by year, whereas Jesus' eschatological kind of religious consciousness is fiercely committed to the Now-Moment in which the self becomes itself by committing itself. Jesus' teaching shows how religious action can be fully this worldly and *historical* action; whereas the Temple's idea of action, liturgical action, is merely the cyclical reenactment of a myth. It is scarcely *human* action at all, for it goes nowhere and achieves nothing.

Why? And how is it that, in Christianity in particular, the Church ended up with its heart outside history altogether and lost in the world of myth? The answer lies in the Grand Narrative of cosmic fall and redemption which Christianity developed and to which it remains firmly attached. In the myth, cosmic history is divided up into a series of stages or dispensations, each of which is an 'Act' in the cosmic drama that God is directing. These dispensations include Paradise, the Patriarchal period, the age of the Mosaic Law, the age of the Gospel or the years of Grace, and finally the Millennium which begins with the return of Christ in glory. During each dispensation human beings live under and are subject to a fixed set of religious conditions which define how things are for them during that period. The change from one dispensation to the next that moves the whole cosmic drama on to its next stage cannot be brought about by human agency, but requires a special act of God. Such special acts of God include, for example, the expulsion of Adam and Eve from Eden which brings about the transition from the Paradisal Age to the Age of the patriarchs; the giving of the Law to Moses which brings about the transition from the Patriarchal Age to the period of the Law; the birth, death and resurrection of Jesus, followed by the gift of the Spirit at Pentecost, which brings about the transition from the years of the Law to the Age of Grace, the period of the Church on earth; and the Second Coming of Christ, which brings about the end of the Church Militant and the beginning of the Millennial Kingdom of Christ and his saints on earth.

I recite the barest outline of the once familiar grand narrative in order to make one vital point. Although it is in a sense true that 'Christianity is an historical religion' which comes to express its whole theology in the form of a vast cosmic story of fall and redemption, we must also note that history is here regarded as a great story not of any *human* endeavours, but simply of the saving acts of *God*. God is almost the only historical agent. The *only* human acts which are vital hinges in the story are the disobedience of Adam, and its exact counterpart, the meritorious obedience of Christ. Marian enthusiasts will also chip in here, wanting to interpolate a reference to the meritorious obedience of Mary, who accepts the role assigned to her in the economy of redemption. But apart from these points, the fact of course remains that God is the Lord of history who has fixed the limits under which we must live until the end of the present dispensation. Latin orthodoxy was always predestinarian: God has foreordained all events. As the director of all directors, God is much more of an *auteur* than Alfred J. Hitchcock ever was.[3]

From all this it follows that classical Latin theology had no idea at all of history as a communal *human* production, and was very pessimistic about the ordinary course of our secular historical life. Nothing we do can make any real difference. We cannot of ourselves change any of the basic conditions of human existence by historical action: we must simply wait for the next dispensation to begin with the Second Coming of Christ. And that is why, as Christian theology developed, Christians withdrew from history and came to spend most of their energy on the annual liturgical round of feasts and fasts commemorating the various key episodes in the cosmic redemption drama. That is why, to this day, the main thing Christians do is 'go to church', at Christmas, Easter, Whitsun and so on, and why preachers put their main effort into interpreting the various events of 'the Christian Year'. Nobody dares to ask, what are we doing all this *for*?

In an interesting comment on these issues, Julian Roberts rightly points out that classical Protestantism was still more pessimistic about the prospects for human historical action than was Roman Catholicism:

> Quite how much of Christ's influence remains in the world after his departure and before his final return is a matter of doctrine. Tridentine Romanism has tended to teach that Christ is present on this earth in the Church

and in his Vicar, the Pope. Protestantism, on the other hand, has usually emphasized the total abandonment of this earth by Christ, and the futility of any attempt to identify his presence here. The ethical and political state of mind induced by this latter doctrine was described by Walter Benjamin as 'melancholy', and analysed in detail in *The Origin of German Tragic Drama*. Only the Protestant attitude is truly Messianic: the Romanist view is something of a mixture.

And in talking about what he describes as 'the Messianic view of history', Roberts, who is writing especially about German thought, adds:

> The point about Messianism is its emphasis on rupture and discontinuity. For Messianism, the arrival of the Messiah is a completely indispensable condition of 'history'. Before the Messiah, we are in a condition of nature, lost to a meaningless mechanism. After the Messiah, we are free – free from natural constraint. There is no intermediate stage between the two epochs … the depravity of the first epoch is so total, and the salvation of the second so complete, that nothing is really the same in both. The individual, as Kierkegaard and the evangelical Christians say, has to be reborn. The implication of this (for many thinkers) . . . was that rationality was *also* tainted.[4]

That is all very illuminating, and helps us once again to see how Christianity became the *opposite* of Jesus – and I refer here of course to Jesus the Jewish teacher, who was very gradually rediscovered during the twentieth century. For we are suddenly reminded that Jesus has no worked out theology of sin and redemption, and as a teacher belongs more to the Wisdom tradition of the Jews than to the history-of-salvation tradition. He is not a grand-narrativist. He doesn't want us to disappear out of history and into church, where we will spend our lives annually recycling the great Christian redemption myth. Instead, he takes from Messianism the idea of a coming Moment when everything is going to become different, and then puts all his emphasis upon our being watchful and actively *seizing* that Moment. It is by this route that he steps clear of Messianism, for he gives eschatological significance to our individual *human* moral decision and action.

The Church says, 'Of yourself you can change nothing. Come and be a worshipper'. Jesus says: 'You can commit yourself to life in way that is like living at the end of the world. When we live like that we begin to change ourselves; we begin to change everything'.

The radical wing of the Protestant Reformation sought to go beyond the Church and to seize the Kingdom. Inevitably, it soon became morally very active, and politically revolutionary – which shows that radical Christianity is indeed highly 'historical'. Horrified, the church protestants and the godly princes repressed it by force. But this is still the territory that needs to be moved into next.

Solar Action

I n our own age, the reformation project that we are discussing – the project of going beyond church Christianity, and instead aiming directly for the last stage of Christianity's historical development as originally scheduled – this project has a very specific meaning. It means thinking about how people may be enabled to create and to find religious meaning and value in the fully wired up and globalized human world of the future.

It is a strange thought that, although the Radical Christian dream of pressing on from the Church to the Kingdom was crushed at the time of the Reformation, the dream of 'Jerusalem' at the end of history – a world of universal well-being with humans globally reconciled and fully transparent to each other – the dream of such a world has continued to work in the Western mind since the seventeenth century, and has inspired all the varieties of utopian, visionary politics. Today it looks closer to fulfilment than ever. It is 'Jerusalem', it is 'America', it is the Promised Land, the Kingdom of Ends, Anarchism and Socialism. Today it takes a somewhat secularized form, as the expectation that the future will bring a globalized eco-humanism so intensely communicative that it will almost generate a single world consciousness in which each of us is a single brain cell.

What will this world be like? Will it be a nightmare – 'totalitarian schlock', an American writer has called it – or might it be made so rich in symbolic meaning and in value that people can see it as the Kingdom of God, at last established on earth? The question is a very big one, simply because of the way the non-arrival of the Kingdom has hung over the entire history of Christianity so far.

The main points are familiar to readers of the New Testament. It has long been agreed that Jesus' mission was not to 'found the church', and still less to furnish the Papacy with its credentials. Jesus did not see himself as having come in order to make bishops important. He was not that kind of figure at all: he was in fact a prophet of the Kingdom of God. That is, he expected the imminent coming of a major world upheaval. There would be a final battle between the forces of good and evil, out of which would come the establishment of a whole new world order, an age of universal well-being or salvation. But he died without seeing the new age that he hoped for, and because it was delayed the church evolved as a stopgap. Its historical task was to gather together a large band of people, 'elect from every nation', and keep them in an orderly, disciplined, expectant posture, ready to move in and take over when the New World finally came. Sometimes the church would compare itself with an army on the march, like ancient Israel marching through the wilderness towards the Promised Land. In this army the clergy were the officer class, and the laity were the foot soldiers.

The church was thus marching towards a great future Event, for which it was preparing its members. Doctrine was about that event, and the certainty of its coming was thought to justify the authority of the clergy and the strict discipline they imposed. But the whole apparatus of the clergy, church law and doctrine, and the great distinction between sacred things (things to do with the church and the new age of final salvation), and the profane world around – all that apparatus would remain in place during the period of transition only, and would vanish when the new age actually arrived. Intellectual and social conditions in the new age would be very different from what they had been in the church. The church and its ways of thinking would then happily pass away. God would no longer be perceived as a distinct being, because the divine would have fully returned into people in a way that is symbolized by the Eucharist and by Pentecost.

Unfortunately, the Kingdom did not come. It was delayed and delayed, until finally its realization was deferred into the heavenly world after death. Now it began to look as if the era of the church 'militant here on earth' would continue for as long as human life continued. Christ was seemingly not going to return to earth within any foreseeable future: he was going to remain in Heaven. This meant that religious attention became firmly focussed on the heavenly world and the church's job was now to get people ready, not for the Kingdom of God on earth, but for Judgement after death. The church had the authority to give you a valid ticket to Heaven, an enormous power to hold. Thus the dictatorship of the church over its members became established in perpetuity, very much as in the history of the Communist party the period of absolute government and ideological tyranny, 'the dictatorship of the proletariat', seemed to become permanent as the hoped for communist society on earth receded further and further into the far future.

In effect, I am saying, the Church came to believe that its own earthly authority was absolute and perpetual as it ceased to believe that it would ever have to hand over to the coming Kingdom. So what was originally scheduled to be only a temporary state of discipline became a permanent yoke, and belief in church dogma became in perpetuity 'necessary for salvation'.

In which case, why the decline of religion? In the case of the collapse of communism what happened was that people stopped believing in the eschatological promise: that is, they didn't believe that the hugely powerful state apparatus would ever voluntarily dissolve itself and allow the ideal world of the communist society to come into being. Suddenly they discovered the *real* saving truth, which is that the whole horrible tyranny is only as strong as your own belief in it. You have only to withhold your assent, and it will collapse. So it did.

The case of the church is rather different, because the justification of the church's claims and its authority has come to lie on the far side of death. Surely, for as long as people continue to die and to be fearful about what may await them after death, the church's claims cannot be decisively falsified? Surely people will go on indefinitely fearing that it might all be true, and they will go on calling in the priest as death approaches?

In order now to move the argument forward, we must go back to the beginning of the argument and cast the net wider. We have to go back almost 3000 years, to the period when the Zoroastrian or Mazdaist theology was taking shape.[1]

It was apparently the Zoroastrian priests of ancient Persia who first developed the idea of world history as a history of salvation, a long drama of Fall and Redemption in several acts. They saw the good god, Ahura Mazda, as having created the world to be the stage on which he would fight his long battle against the powers of evil, and they held that his final victory would be seen on earth:

> The last days will be marked by increasing wretchedness and cosmic calamities. Then the World Saviour, the Saoshyant, will come in glory. He is to be born of the seed of the prophet, miraculously preserved within a lake, and a virgin mother. There will be a great battle between . . . good men and bad, ending in victory for the good. The bodies of those who have died earlier will be resurrected and united with their souls, and the

Last Judgement will take place . . . the saved will be given ambrosia to eat, and their bodies will become as immortal as their souls. The kingdom of Ahura Mazda will come on an earth made perfect again, and the blessed will rejoice everlastingly in his presence.[2]

Such is perhaps the original eschatological myth, the story of the last days, the last battle, the last Trump, the Last Judgement and the establishment of a millennial kingdom of universal bliss and salvation here on a renewed earth. It has had a huge influence on the Jews, who perhaps picked it up during their Babylonian captivity. Modern Sionism is a late outworking of the ancient hope. Through the Israelite prophets it passed to Jesus and to Christianity, to Islam and then more recently to Western historicism and political utopianism. It even influenced the eschatologies of Hinduism and Buddhism. It is prominent in the early history of North America, itself 'the new world', and was central to the hopes of anarchists and communists. The last famous expressions of it were Martin Luther King's statement of the American dream in the 1960s, and John Lennon's lyric 'Imagine' in the 1970s.

Over a very long period most of humanity, and especially the Western half of it, have been deeply influenced by this great story. Above all, it is the story that delivered people from the tyranny of traditionalism. It first gave us the idea that the future might be, could be, *would* be better than the past. Instead of being forever confined to standards and patterns of behaviour laid down in a past Golden Age, people could look forward in hope to a better world yet to come. More than that, they are invited to imagine what a better world might be like. It becomes, not just an object of aspiration, but also possibly a goal of action. By the way you lived you could do a little more than just ready yourself for the new world: you could actually expedite its coming. At least, you could begin to realize its values. This invites the new thought that religion may come to be seen as our human way of first imagining new values and a better world, and then actually working to bring them into being. Religion: our communal way of reimagining and reinventing ourselves, and projecting our values.

This process of world remaking takes a long time – or at least *has* taken a long time, hitherto. To see why, consider the fact that many of the principal structural features of the coming better world have been surprisingly constant, if not quite from Zoroaster to John Lennon, then certainly from the prophet Isaiah to Karl Marx and modern times. I shall simply set out the leading features, in the hope that for the most part I do not need to give more than the briefest biblical references.

First, in the better world (of the Kingdom of Heaven, or the communist society), religion no longer exists as a separate institution and sphere of life because its task in that role has been completed. Instead, *all of life becomes a sacred continuum.* God is scattered into everyone and, politically, monarchy is replaced by democracy. All hierarchy and distinctions of social rank disappear, just as the distinction between the sacred and the profane disappears.[3]

Secondly, and in close connection with these changes, because there is no longer any value outside life, *all value in life becomes intrinsic.* When we come to the last world, the world at the end of the world, the world at the end of history, then there is no further reality beyond the here and now, and therefore there is no instrumental value. There is no instrumental action, because there is no longer any better future to be looked forward to. We no longer act for the sake of some future and long-term good, such as the liberation of humanity, or the salvation of our own souls. Everything must be valued and affirmed and loved and done just for its own sake, and in the here and now: no ethical theory is needed, because we feel no need to justify our valuations. And as there is no instrumentality, so there is no concealment or deception. You can't have ulterior motives when nothing is ulterior – there is no 'Beyond' – any more. All communication becomes completely open and transparent; daylight is perpetual and fills everything.[4] You become serene, like an old person who no longer has a future to worry about and work for.

Thirdly, in the new world people will not be under the yoke of any external authority or written law. Instead, everything flows from the heart. There is no moral realism (that is, there is no real external moral standard), and instead the only basis for ethics will be our newly realized full co-humanity. In effect, *ethics becomes purely humanitarian.* All life becomes a flow of exchange, called in religious language 'communion', and in modern language 'communication'.[5]

And fourthly, as human beings become fully reconciled to each other and to their world, the world becomes fully appropriated to humans. St Paul makes the point by saying simply: All things are yours. The physical world and the human social world coincide. *Human culture becomes fully globalized.* The misunderstanding caused by language differences and the conflict caused by ethnic differences disappears. There is a hint of some form of world government.[6]

To repeat these four main points, in the new era all of life becomes a single sacred continuum, all value in life becomes intrinsic, ethics becomes purely humanitarian, and human consciousness becomes fully globalized. And these four points can very easily be illustrated in detail from the Israelite prophets, from the teaching of Jesus in the synoptic Gospels, and from other New Testament books such as the Acts of the Apostles, and the Revelation of John. And the same themes are still being appealed to by twentieth-century people.

How far have the churches as we know them ever actually sought to create the new world as thus described? The early church is reported to have tried: it broke out of the ancient Jewish sacrificial system, tried to overcome the received clean/unclean distinction, sought to create a fully reciprocally transparent society, welcomed gentile members, and sought to practise humanitarian ethics by redistribution to the poor.[7] But the original impulse faded, as the church gradually turned into a salvation machine dispensing sacramental Grace to people who were preparing their souls for death. Then, in much later times, certain radical groups which emerged at the Reformation made a fresh effort to put the original programme into effect. The Quakers are the outstanding example: they abolished the whole religious sphere of life (the church, the clergy and the sacraments); they affirmed the value of life, to the point of being strict practitioners of non-violence; they were the chief pioneers of our modern humanitarian ethics; and they sought to be politically supranational. The conclusion is unavoidable: if in the original logic of Western religious thought all religious action is ultimately aimed at bringing in the new world, then the Quakers have been the most thoroughgoing Christians.

To return now to today's church and to the decline of religion, how are we to interpret the present situation in the West? I hope that my conclusion will already have occurred to you. It is that since the Enlightenment secular culture in the West has continued to move steadily on towards the historical realization of the ancient religious dream. It has gone very much farther than the church. For example, Western secular culture is much more egalitarian and democratic than the church, and more consistent in its respect for human rights. Secular culture has become much more globalized and supranational, while the church too often has become merely national and lost in admiration for its own past. Very strikingly, secular culture has recently ceased to believe in progress and has effectively ceased to believe in life after death. It therefore knows that we already live in the last world, and that there will not be any further world beyond this one. Secular culture is therefore already committing itself to the here and now, to the value of life and to the new religion of life.[8] Thus religion becomes more serious when we stop believing in life after death. In addition, the 'ecumenical' attempt to build a new and globalized world order, a United Nations, and a range of international institutions, has gone much further in the secular sphere than it has in the churches. Humanitarian ethics of the 'Kingdom' type is much more developed in the work of an organization like Medecins sans Frontières than it is anywhere in the churches. And finally, secular culture is becoming intensely communicative on a global scale, and is much more committed to freedom of speech than is the church.

I conclude from all this that in the Western tradition secular culture has since the Enlightenment continued to pursue the ancient religious dream of a new world at the end of historical time, and with considerable success. The world it has been building, the world of the United Nations, international law, democratic politics, ceaseless global communication and humanitarian ethics, a world now committed to the struggle for the emancipation of women and the reconciliation of ethnic and religious differences – this new world of ours represents a very much further developed version of the original Christian programme than anything available from the churches.

Here we find the reason for the so-called 'decline of religion'. It might be better called the redundancy of the church, if it is indeed the case that by the church's own criteria what it thinks of as 'the world' is now becoming much more truly Christian than is the church itself. The church has been left in the past, as Christianity has moved out of it and has continued to develop in the larger world outside.

All this raises in a very pointed way the question of just what it is that religion is *for*. In the modern West religion seems to the average lay person to be about two things, credal belief and churchgoing. One assents and adheres to a system of supernatural beliefs, and one joins with the church in observing the annual liturgical cycle through which the beliefs are enacted and celebrated. But why? None of this nowadays makes any very conspicuous difference to the way people live, and all the manifest facts about the world and life and death and culture are just the same for believers and unbelievers alike. So what is the point of the ecclesiastical type of religion? What does it accomplish? What do people get from it?

It is hard to avoid Schopenhauer's view that ecclesiastical faith is principally about the fear of death. The presumption must be that very many people continue to be afraid of dying and of what they think may be in store for them beyond death. For Roman Catholics in particular, it seems to be the church's ministrations at the time of death that are the most highly valued.

There are however some very uncomfortable corollaries of this view of religion. People who spend their lives preparing for death fail to make the best of this, our only life. When people finally give up belief in any sort of life after death, they will begin to see *this present life* as final, and as religiously precious. They will begin to disdain death oriented religion, and look instead for a kind of religion that will enable them to make the most of this life while we have it. And it is exactly this switch of religious interest towards this present life that characterizes the modern religious scene. In Britain, for example, even death itself is now approached in a life centred way: the funeral service is increasingly renamed *A Thanksgiving for the Life of* . . . and the memorial service is renamed *A Celebration of the Life of* . . .

The alternative view of the purpose of religion goes back, as we have seen, to ancient eschatological belief. Religious thought was imaginative and utopian. People saw the practice of religion as a way of preparing for, and perhaps as a way of hastening, the final earthly conflict between the powers of good and evil and the coming of a new age on earth at the end of historical time. Religion is not primarily about supernatural belief, but about hope. It is our communal way of generating dreams of how we and our life and our world might be made better. We prepare ourselves for the dream, and we start to think about how we might actually start to make it all come true.

My suggestion has been that the so-called 'decline of religion' is people's abandonment en masse of the kind of ecclesiastical religion that concentrated upon promising comfort and reassurance in the face of death. Instead, we should see religious thought and practice as imaginative and utopian. Religion is a communal way of reimagining and remaking the self and the world. It is about what we are to live *by* and what we are to live *for*. At a time when political thought is very unadventurous, and when the world is becoming overwhelmingly dominated by technology, we need religion as much as ever. We need it as a human, value creating *activity*. Hence the shape of the new Reformation: I am describing it as being a switch from Church to Kingdom, and as a switch away from seeing the self as an immortal spiritual substance that is busy purifying itself and preparing for death, to a new 'Kingdom' view of selfhood as solar process, continually pouring itself out into symbolic expression and passing away. Our task is to inject religious meaning and value into our own bit of the common human world and so make, each one of us, our contribution to the whole.

That is what I mean by solar action, but I need to deal briefly with a common objection, which is perhaps best made by quoting two examples from fiction: in Brian Moore's *No Other Life* the young black priest, Jean-Paul Cantave, known as Jeannot, is a charismatic incantatory preacher influenced by Liberation theology. He takes the side of the poor on his desperately backward Caribbean island, and his oratory carries him to the presidency on a wave of popular enthusiasm. But he is a visionary, and he has neither time nor patience for the hard graft of practical politics. His régime soon fails, and he flees into hiding. To the poor he seemed to be almost a Messiah. They mythicize him, but he was a failure.

Something similar is apt to happen to idealistic young schoolteachers in D.H. Lawrence's novels, and in particular it happens to Ursula in *The Rainbow*.[9] Her large class of children present to her a wall of suspicion and latent hostility. She thinks she can win them over by her charm, her sincere goodwill and her youth – but she can't. In schoolteaching there is always a battle of wills, and a teacher needs *craft* in both senses of that word: professional skill and low cunning. So Ursula fails, as Jeannot fails. Nothing lasting can be done or built in the world by enthusiasm alone. One must work hard at acquiring and exercising the relevant skills and practical wisdom. In politics, those who are merely saints are merely a nuisance.

This argument has been brought in recent years against my talk of 'solar ethics'. People have taken me to be extolling ardent reckless expressionists like Vincent van Gogh, who for two or three years touched the heights and produced a glorious vision of the world – and then burnt out and died. Such an artist becomes very widely loved and very precious to us, but he was a casualty. We are glad to have a few such people, but one cannot wish that everyone could be like that.

I agree. Solar ethics has been misunderstood. It was first introduced not as a moral panacea, but as a 'spirituality' – that is, as a way of relating oneself to life that conquers the fear of death.[10] In the past people usually had a very supernaturalist idea of the Kingdom of God, and they believed that in it human beings living on this earth and in time would have the original 'natural immortality' of Adam and Eve restored to them. Today, obviously, we cannot believe anything like that. There is no other life, and we humans will always be mortals who live in time. So I produced *solar ethics* in order to show how a person who lives in time and knows she's mortal can nevertheless have eternal life and enjoy the very highest religious happiness. For me solar ethics makes possible earthly happiness, unpoisoned by the fear of misfortune and death. I hope that in the future it will be taught and practised by people of every kind, including – why not? – administrators and technologists.

One World

Chapter Sixteen

Only quite recently, and after a very long, drawn-out delaying action, have we begun fully and openly to admit that there is only one world – this world, *our* world. We don't live in the outer suburbs of reality, whence we look to an independent Centre outside our region towards which we gravitate and from which our lives are controlled, because it is now clear to us that all this, around us, is all there is. The proximate is ultimate: what is nearest to us is also final for us. This, in every possible way, is *it*.

The realization that there is only one world comes to us with all the more force because it has come on no less than four levels at once. We don't believe in any form of *life after death*; we don't believe in *a hidden, controlling supernatural* order which may at any time intervene in the affairs of this world to reveal itself to us or to help us; we are not *platonists* who believe that as well as the world of sense objects there is also a distinct, unchanging world of thought objects; and we don't believe in *progress*: that is, the old talk about the ultimate conquest of nature and the perfectibility of man has given place to a sober realization that we will be doing well if, very soon, we can get ourselves into a stable relationship with our natural environment.

Some people will want to object that in some of these areas serious disputes are still going on. There are still mathematical platonists, for example, who claim that mathematical truth is discovered and not invented. The formalists don't yet have it all their own way. And there are still cosmological realists, who believe that our natural science does more than just *impute* a mathematical order to the world: it copies or traces a preexistent and mind-independent world order that exists out there. However, in philosophy one cannot and one does not wait until all the arguments are over and the matter is wholly beyond dispute. So I simply assert that it has now become clear to us, on several different levels, that there is only one world. Everything is immanent, everything is interconnected, everything is contingent – and somehow, everything is channelled through us.

This last point, radical humanism, is best grasped by understanding how and why it is that our language is the best image of our world. I write on the very day that the completion of the first draft of the human genome is being announced. Some of the commentary implies that the genome already existed out there *as information* – as indeed a *text* that was waiting to be deciphered and read by us. But that is of course not what has happened: what's happened is rather that the first, slightly rough draft of the whole genome has been *expressed as text* by scientists and published by them on the Internet so that it is now common knowledge. Realists think we have *decoded* the genome, but we haven't: we've *encoded* it, expressing it as a chain of signs.

It is in this way that by our use of language we appropriate the world, structure it, and make it our world, *the known world*. The business of everyday life is transacted very largely – indeed, almost entirely – in language together with more specialized forms of symbolic communication, and this continual trading back and forth of language is what builds and maintains the world of everyday life. The specialized vocabularies of our various branches of knowledge and so on are added on around the edges of ordinary language, and visited as required.

This makes it possible to see what is meant by radical humanism, and its suggestion that somehow everything is channelled through us. We know nothing of any view of the world other and bigger than our own, and we cannot operate in any other medium than our language. Anthropocentrism (I mean, putting our small and gossipy selves at the centre of everything) no longer looks *presumptuous*. On the contrary, it is unremarkable because we can scarcely imagine any alternative to it. We are the ones through whom the world becomes world: that is, it is through the movement of our language that we appropriate the world, making it ours, structuring it and making it *bright*, making it known *as* world, our common public world, the *known* world.[1]

Philosophically, then, it is we through whom the world has become known and fully itself. What is wonderful about our natural science is not that we have managed to make copies of various bits of an already laid on world structure, but rather that through us, through our communicative activity, the world has become organized, bright and known as world.

By making it ours we have finished the world, which suggests a general rule that every world – and also every subworld – actually *needs* a subject or subjects whose world it is. In England there is a slightly archaic expression, *the fancy*, used to signify the community of people who are devoted to horse racing, or dog breeding, or pigeon fancying or whatever. In each case the fans' shared enthusiasm generates a little world, structures it, imputes value to fancied objects, and so on. Thus we humans are natural world builders, and in a way that oddly reminds us of the old Christian belief that Christ, who is God's uttered speech and also is the universal Man, was God's agent in the creation of the world. So the world is indeed made through a Man! Once again we see that ancient theological ideas, bizarre when read realistically, suddenly make sense when we get into the way of reading them non-realistically. Yes indeed, there is a sense in which we humans make the world: Kant was the first modern philosopher to say so. And the old metaphysical belief that a world needs a creator can be swapped for its more up-to-date counterpart: a world is a sort of environment or stage setting, and every world needs at least someone whose world it is in order to be a world.

This picture of the relationship between world, language and humans emerges clearly in and from the work of the two chief philosophers of the twentieth century, Wittgenstein and Heidegger. From it we see clearly not only that there is only one big world, the known world, but also what it means to say that somehow everything is channelled through us. We are the bit of the world in which the world becomes aware of itself. We are locked to our language and our world just as much as our language and our world are locked to us. 'Everything is immanent, everything is interconnected, everything is contingent', I wrote above: now I add– 'including us'. Mysteriously, we ourselves are bits of the *all this* that becomes conscious of itself *as* all this only in us, through our language. Writing down this last sentence, I feel philosophical vertigo, because we have crashed together, in a rather Buddhist fashion, a pair of seeming opposites. Everything is utterly mundane, everything is here and now; and yet also Everything is final. Everything passes, and everything in passing passes away finally. Everything is chance, but everything chance is also a last chance, slipping away.

That the passing moment is also a religiously final Now-moment is a familiar theme in the history of religion, best known perhaps for its occurrence in Buddhist writing from Nagarjuna to Dogen, and in the Western tradition from Jesus to Eckhart and Blake. In the Bible and in Kierkegaard the Now-moment is above all the time of choice and decision: 'Choose you this day whom you will serve . . . Behold, now is the acceptable time, now is the day of salvation'.[2] The theme is familiar. It's a cliché. But it returns with much greater force when we finally admit to ourselves that we have lost all ideas of locating life's goal (or, as people say, its 'meaning') in another and Better World beyond this world. Our world really is outsideless. There is nothing after death, nothing up above, and nothing in the future that is going to draw everything together and make sense of it all. No immanent purpose carries us towards a future consummation of everything. In which case, as Nietzsche sees clearly, we must find and affirm what we live for nowhere else but Now, in the present moment. In the older teachers, the appeal to the Now-moment as the time to decide, or the time to experience Nirvana, had an optional air about it. There were other more gradual paths that the teacher might invoke. But now there aren't. We are literally on our last legs, in our last hours, and we will never be better able to see and seize the Truth than we are now.

Hence the shift to kingdom theology and solar living. We give up the old ecclesiastical longtermism (which was open to criticism even in its own day, and on its own terms) and instead commit ourselves as ardently as we can to our life in its very transience, making the most of each moment.

The poet Robert Graves in his lengthy old age used to compare our life with a bunch of grapes. We hold it up by the stalk, so that the bunch hangs downwards. Then the grapes are eaten from the top down, and 'the next one you eat is always the best that you have left'. That is a pagan, aesthetic way of putting it. Following Jesus, I have suggested that solar living is an ethical reading of the same image. Never procrastinate, because you have only a finite quantity left, and there will never come a better opportunity than this one. Live life to the full, *now*: give it all you've got, *now*.

Inevitably, someone is sure to say once again that Cupitt's unbelief sounds more religious than normal people's belief; but that is the kind of muddle from which I am trying to escape. *Of course* the loss of dogmatic belief – that is, the end of ecclesiastical deferral – makes religion come alive again. You should see that by now: ecclesiastical religion offered us deferral and interim dogmatic belief, not as *being* true religion, but only as a *substitute* for true religion. Now the substitute no longer works, and we find ourselves obliged to discover the real thing.

Chapter
Seventeen

The Dream of a
Perfect Society

In or soon after 387 B.C.E. Plato established a school on the outskirts of Athens, close by a grove sacred to Academus. This school, the so-called 'Academy', survived as a visible focus and exponent of the platonic tradition for the next eight centuries, until it was finally shut down by the Emperor Justinian in C.E. 529.

While it lasted the Academy functioned as a sort of 'church' of platonism, and many of its heads, including Plotinus, Porphyry and Proclus, were important figures in their day. Inevitably, it was they who developed Plato's own philosophy into 'neo-platonism', a body of doctrine adapted to the cultural conditions of the later Roman Empire – because where there is a church, it has to keep up to date.

When the Academy was closed, platonism was no longer represented by an official church that taught it, and there was no longer a 'pope' of platonism in the person of the Academy's current head. But of course platonism did not die. It flourishes to the present day, not least because the subtle dialectics of Plato's own writings can be better appreciated when there is not a 'pope' who puts out a current official interpretation of Plato. Platonism does better *without* a church.

Something similar is true of Buddhism. It seems disorganized and plural. It is a very large loose knit family of local traditions, sects and occasional brilliant individuals. It is supple, adapting itself readily to different cultural settings; and the result is that Buddhism in the modern West is like penetrating oil. It gets everywhere, loosening up our thinking, changing us effortlessly. Its lack of organization is a big advantage.

And what of Christianity? Until the fifteenth century or so the word was hardly used. There was simply the Church, which was an immensely powerful organization with a highly developed ideology and legal system. The theology did various jobs, articulating the church's faith, spelling out what it required of and promised to its members, and above all, defining the church vis-à-vis the rest of humankind. For Christians, as for Jews and Muslims, the distinction between the holy people and the surrounding world of gentiles or unbelievers is fundamental. Most people in the modern West will have noticed the extent to which many Muslims, Jews and certain Orthodox and Evangelical Christians want to talk about the fortunes, and especially the *mis*fortunes, of their own people. There is a word, 'ethnocentric', for people who are preoccupied with their own ethnic differentia; but we do not seem to have a word for people whose view of life and attitude to other people is dominated by their own religious allegiance. (Should it be 'fideicentric'?) For such a person the first question of all is invariably: 'Are you one of us, or are you an outsider, and therefore a potential threat to us?' For them, it is always wartime and they must know right away whether you are their friend or foe. Specially developed antennae enable them very quickly to divine the correct answer to their question, and all their subsequent behaviour towards you is governed by it.

Ecclesiastical Christianity of course tends to be like that – but kingdom Christianity is not. Ecclesiastical Christianity is the church, and it implants in every one of its members a dualistic ideology that divides all of reality at every level between the City of God (the Church) and the City of Man (secular society), the faithful and the heathen, the saved and the lost, Grace and Nature, God and Satan, and so forth. The whole theology is designed to keep a great Army together as it marches through the potentially hostile territory of this present world. But in the kingdom era there is no longer a clear and sharp distinction between the sacred and secular realms, and the old fiercely dualistic and indeed *oppositional* ways of thinking no longer seem appropriate at all. The whole world of secular life and knowledge has been hugely enlarged, diversified and revalued, and the sacred is now scattered across it.[1] The result is that we find ourselves living in a time when the Church is ill at ease in society because her traditional dualistic outlook and theology are no longer appropriate. In secular society Christianity seems to have become a pervasive cultural influence that is still developing and finding new expressions in art, morality and politics; but the Church is unhappily stuck in a time warp with nothing useful to say. Too often, the Church gives the impression of being composed of naysayers, killjoys who disapprove of far too much of the world about them. It seems that Christianity still functions very happily as an invisible, ubiquitous moral and imaginative influence, but that its visible organized form is now redundant. We no longer have any use for the old sharp contrasts between *the church* and *the world*, the sacred and the profane, and so on.

The hypothesis for consideration, then, is this: that in the kingdom era which has now begun Christianity no longer needs to be embodied in a distinct institution over against the rest of culture. Like 'platonism' or 'Buddhism', it now seems to do better as an ubiquitous presence or influence within the general flow of cultural life. But it must be admitted right away that this suggestion will alarm many people, because the church has meant so much to so many for so long. The church claims to have the power to issue valid passports to heaven. The church has been, or has purported to be, a divinely instituted and guaranteed society to which one can and should unreservedly commit one's whole life, including even one's intellect and one's conscience. The church's teachings are to be simply obeyed. Sooner or later every other society will disappoint you, but Holy Mother Church is endlessly patient and will never let you down.

It is hard to bring out the point here with sufficient force, but if you have ever been emotionally captivated by the idea of a perfect society, a society that really *does* have all the answers to the greatest questions, and that really is entitled to promise you absolute security, then you have been touched by an idea that cannot be given up without pain. That's obvious. Since the 1830s or so, large numbers of thinking people in successive generations have found themselves 'losing their faith' and seemingly compelled to break with the church. Most of them have found the break extremely painful, and it presented them with a dilemma. They might see no alternative to the position that Wittgenstein once described to Con Drury: 'We have to live without the consolation of belonging to a church'. Or they might cling obstinately to the dream of a perfect society and a great good cause to which one can commit oneself unreservedly, and in which one can find absolute security – but look for the dream's fulfilment somewhere else, outside the church.

The desire to find a satisfactory replacement for the church has been very strong. It has typically expressed itself in various forms of political messianism, of which the most important of all has been, perhaps, the idea of 'America'. America has been the dream of a New World, an unspoilt land where refugees from the cruelties of ecclesiastical Christianity could hope to establish a truly free Christian society and embark upon the great task of building the Kingdom of God on earth. Arguably, 'America' and kingdom Christianity are one and the same thing, to an extent that helps to explain why to this day citizens of the United States still have a uniquely strong (and in some ways even *justified*) belief in their own country. But, to avoid misunderstanding, I should emphasize that I am not praising the rather unremarkable versions of church Christianity that are established in the modern USA. What I am praising, and describing as Kingdom Christianity, is the *secular* tradition in America, the separation of church and State, the belief in religious freedom, and the older versions of the American dream. So we are not talking about American puritanism and pietism, and we are not talking about the USA as a powerful nation state which like other nation states behaves as a rational egoist in its overseas relations: we are talking about the dream of 'America', a beacon land that is not only post-ecclesiastical, but therewith is also 'pentecostal' and post-national; a new kind of society, built on the idea of freedom.

America is by no means the only example of a post-ecclesiastical 'dream' society in which one may try to find a post-religious fulfilment of ancient eschatological hopes: but the two examples that come first to mind, Soviet Russia and the State of Israel, are both of them ambivalent and even tragic.

Russia has known several distinct waves of messianism, Tsarist, panslavist and Marxist-Leninist. Russia is Holy Russia, and Moscow is the Third Rome. Russia's Imperial and ecclesiastical messianism is a wholly second-millennium creation, the Patriarchate of Moscow dating only from 1589, and effective caesaropapism from the reign of Peter the Great (1676–1725). In the nineteenth century a messianism of Russia, her church, her soul and her sufferings flourished along with panslavism, at the same time as the thoroughly secularized messianism of Karl Marx was also beginning to make itself felt. In the twentieth century, during the Soviet period, the Communist Party's attempts to create a planned utopia within the old Russian Empire invited comparison with the Jesuit 'reductions' in Paraguay and with the way the Monastic Order (that is, the Benedictines) had earlier organized the agricultural peasantry in Western Europe. At the height of the confrontation of the Superpowers in the 1960s and 1970s, *both* the USA and Russia could with some plausibility claim to be the beacon country, *lux gentium*, the last best hope of humankind; and *both* could claim that their inspiring hope was a form of kingdom Christianity.

And now today Russia is a land dying of drink and despair, overtaken by a catastrophe of awesome proportions. In Russia they did not put freedom first: the dream was always to be realized by 'strong leadership' – that is, by force.

Israel is another example of a messianic 'dream' country in which we see a paradoxical and post-religious realization of ancient religious hopes. For many in Jewry the Holocaust was a religious disaster on a scale that made old style realistic belief in the Jewish God no longer possible, and the proclamation of the State of Israel in 1948 could therefore not be read as a fulfilment of the ancient hope of a Restoration of Israel *by God*. But secular Jews who knew and loved the old religious tradition could still see in modern Israel a genuine and joyful secular fulfilment of the old religious hope. And the paradox goes further and deeper than that, because the ancient religious hope was always for reconciliation between Israel and her non-Jewish neighbours[2] – a reconciliation that nowadays *only liberal and secular Israelis* are likely to seek and to bring about. The ultra-orthodox want to maintain *separation* between Jew and non-Jew, and refuse to concede land for peace. Thus today ancient Israel's eschatological hopes can be fulfilled only by the secular tradition, and will not be fulfilled by the religious tradition. We are in a period in which it seems that a secularized religious outlook is the only *legitimate* successor of the 'ecclesiastical' religion of the past.

Chapter
Eighteen

Nihilism and Humanitariansim

As we have seen, ecclesiastical religion tends always to be realistic and cosmological: it likes to generate an elaborately structured sacred universe. By contrast, the preacher of kingdom religion seeks to deconstruct the sacred universe and to prepare us for the coming of nihilism, which we are to embrace with religious joy. Now I need to explain a little further how and why nihilism is such a valuable moral and religious purge.

In traditional cultures the world is very commonly thought of as having been created by a series of acts of discrimination or discernment. The two words have a common root in the Latin verb *cernere*, to separate, with special reference to the sifting or sieving by which the wheat is separated from the chaff, and good stuff from rubbish generally. Discrimination or discernment evidently involves evaluation, because it does not simply divide the flux of experience into two equal and similar zones: on the contrary, it seems to *structure* the world, so that two markedly different things or principles or regions appear. One of them is prior, founding, normative and lucid, and the other is its secondary, darker and less stable counterpart or 'Other'. They thus make an asymmetrical, complementary pair: familiar examples from mythology begin with light and darkness, which are usually associated with a whole series of other and closely related pairs: waking and sleeping, consciousness and unconsciousness, Day and Night, Sun and Moon. In the universally familiar Genesis narrative we then hear of Heaven and Earth, Land and Sea, Animals and Plants, and Man and Woman.

Mention of the male-female distinction invites the question: 'Is it true that the way people in the past — and we ourselves in our infancy — have perceived and internalized the sexual difference has come subsequently to act as a model or template for our entire construction of the world? There is some confirmation of this hypothesis in the theogonies of polytheism, where the cosmological pairs are not established by a chain of distinct utterances of the creative Word of one God, but are themselves pairs of divinities, each of which is begotten by its predecessor, and begets its successor. In which case, it is indeed the sexual difference that gives birth to everything else.

We should be wary, however, of the conclusion drawn by some, to the effect that all traditional symbolic thinking, and the whole traditional construction of the world, was nothing but applied sexism. There are too many very awkward exceptions, such as the fact that in ancient Egypt the sky is female, Nut, and the earth male, Geb. To most people that will surely seem horribly wrong way round. It is all wrong that in Egyptian art Geb, on his back, should be straining upwards so awkwardly as he tries to penetrate the sky. And isn't it also horribly *wrong* that in German, which surely ought to be reliably patriarchal, the Sun is feminine? And there are many other such seeming inconsistencies: for example, in our own culture a tradition of portraying Woman as more fickle than Man coexists happily with another tradition that portrays Woman as more virtuous and faithful than Man. We seem quite happy to invoke whichever stereotype suits us at any one moment.

Perhaps then we should change the hypothesis and consider instead the possibility that people everywhere tend to think and to structure their worlds in terms of asymmetrical binary oppositions, a pattern that then gets applied to the human man-woman difference just as it gets applied to everything else. The reason for this is probably (in a *very* broad sense) ethical. Everywhere language is used to advise and admonish, telling people which way round to see everything, which way to go, and what to prefer. Choose this and leave that: there is always a Way of Life and a Way of Death, a right and a wrong, a kernel and a husk, a winner and a loser. Language is cruel: the runner-up, the one that comes second, is the loser, the one whom God 'hates'. 'Is not Esau Jacob's brother? Yet I have loved Jacob but I have hated Esau', says God.[1] But that's the way it has to be. So in traditional society thinking is in terms of asymmetrical binary contrasts, which then generate a world view that embodies and confirms traditional values.

Now we have two possibilities. We may regard the sexual relationship as the original unequal, asymmetrical binary opposition which — endlessly permuted and recycled — becomes the basic building block of all culture and world view. Or alternatively we may say that if the world was originally just a featureless flux, then the mere drawing of a great line across it would not by itself create anything. The drawing of the line must introduce some difference of priority, of power, and of value between right and left; between what's on one side of the line and what's on the other side. *Thus a cosmos cannot be created at all except by establishing unequal, asymmetrical binary contrasts.*[2] For there to be a world, there must be discrimination, and that means discrimination in the hard sense: there is always a loser, always something that comes second. Without that ordering and preference, there doesn't get to be a world at all. In sum: to structure Chaos, inequalities must be imposed. Without inequality, no reality.[3]

On the first of these theories sexism seems to be the chief culprit, and it would seem that if we could create a non-sexist human psychology then we might be able to build a non-sexist Cosmos. But, on the second view, inequality, asymmetry and difference (or '*différance*') are inescapable features of any ordered world – as indeed they are of language itself. For is not meaning itself always produced by prioritizing Something and differentiating it from its Other, that stands just behind it? And are not all words accompanied by their shadowy antonyms, metonyms, correlates, counterparts, so that we always think of back and forth, up and down, right and left, give and take, in and out, before and after, and life and death? Perhaps the bilateral symmetry of our own bodies – and their slight asymmetry, too – is what first sets us thinking this way.

We should further notice that if binary thinking is a pervasive feature of myths and cosmologies, it has played an even greater part in subsequent philosophical and religious thought. Plato is steeped in it, and does not he himself declare that 'matter and form are the mother and father of being'? Because Plato himself is so highly binary, the entire Western philosophical tradition has remained so until modern times. We still use his binary vocabulary of time and eternity, form and matter, being and becoming, appearance and reality, and so on. Similarly, in the religious tradition, thought has always been shaped by very sharp contrasts between the sacred and the profane, the holy and the common, the clean and the unclean, the divine and the human, Holy God and sinful man, Grace and Nature, salvation and damnation, and Heaven and Hell. In many faith traditions, the ritual marking of the distinctions just *is* the practice of religion.

The way this works out in religious thought is neatly illustrated by the Elizabethan Reformed (or Calvinist) writer, William Perkins (1558–1602). In *A Golden Chaine, or the Description of Theology* (1590) Perkins draws the whole Plan of Salvation in a big diagram that shows all cosmic history as a dance of the binaries.[4] The Grand Narrative begins with the eternal decree of election in God's right hand, and the eternal decree of reprobation in God's left hand. It ends with the sealing of Heaven and Hell. In between the beginning and the end of the story everything is black or white, being rigidly controlled by the power of God and by the clarity with which the opposing principles are contrasted and played off against each other. God is, you might say, the Great Discriminator, who makes sure that in the end everything is exposed as being – and as having been all along – either snow white or jet black. As was decreed in the beginning, everything ends up either at God's right hand, or on his left.

The purpose of this discussion so far has been to recall the extent to which, in the Western tradition, we have seen reality as produced by acts of distinction, discrimination, discernment. Great lines were drawn across the primal Chaos, each line bringing into being a complementary unequal pair like light and darkness. By such acts of division and discrimination the world of linguistic meaning was produced, values and disvalues were produced, the Cosmos was ordered, and History was set in motion.

It is evident, then, that the main Western philosophical tradition since Plato, and the main theological tradition at least since the Jewish apocalyptic writings, have both been firmly committed to realism and to discrimination. So we have been committed to a highly unequal world picture, with numerous inbuilt ethical/ontological scales. Notice that the cause of realism and the cause of discrimination – including God's negative discrimination, his just rejection of that which ends up at his left hand – the two causes, I say, are one and the same, for it is discrimination that alone produces reality. The Creator and the Judge are one and the same.

Now I begin to understand why, in the much discussed writings of John Milbank, 'theology' and 'nihilism' are set up as being *themselves* a pair of binary opposites.[5] For him as much as for a Muslim, the great choice is the choice between theological realism and secular nihilism. Milbank recognizes that since about the time of Schelling and Hegel Western thought has been gradually turning away from Plato and has been attempting to transcend, or undo, or 'deconstruct' the great binary oppositions that he imposed upon it. In effect – Milbank is saying – Western philosophy and secular culture have been driving very successfully towards nihilism. But in Milbank's own scheme of thought, nihilism is regarded as a very bad thing. Only theology (and an eclectic sort of catholicized neo-Calvinism at that) can deliver us from it. To speak more plainly, only God can conquer the Nihil at which Western thought has arrived. *Fiat lux*, says God: 'Let there be light'. So God will reinstate the old discriminations, and bring back the good old days.

There are however some very serious objections to the way Milbank describes our present religious and cultural situation. In effect, Milbank identifies the cause of theology with the cause of a highly differentiated sacred cosmology, produced by multiple acts of discrimination. For him and his allies, Christianity was most itself at the peak of the Middle Ages. But we do not live in a world of that type any longer. Our world is now the world as pictured by natural science, and we are energetically fighting our moral battles *against* the various surviving forms of negative discrimination left over from the religious past. Our ethical humanitarianism is magnificently nihilistic: one gives succour to the other simply on the basis of our barest co-humanity and quite *regardless* of race, colour, creed, gender, sexual orientation, doctrinal soundness and moral desert.[6] Thoroughgoing anti-discrimination – i.e., *nihilism* – is 'political correctness', and is what makes our brand of religious humanism so novel and so beautiful. We very consciously do *not* discriminate: that is, we do not even *wish* to classify people and fix their position on various value scales before we agree to minister to them. On the contrary, we remember that in our tradition religion at its best has always yearned to see the end of religion: that is, 'in those days', in the Kingdom of God on earth, in the heavenly world, in the longed for perfect world at the end of the world, the great binary distinctions are undone. There is no longer any chasm between God and man, between the sacred and the profane, between the clean and the unclean, between saints and ordinary citizens, between man and woman, between masters and servants, nor between light and darkness, and the manifest and the hidden, for in the Kingdom of Heaven there are no shadows or concealment, and everything is open and explicit.

The point here is very familiar in the Bible. The prophets and Jesus criticized the sacrificial system and the whole elaborate apparatus of mediated religion. It does not save. It offers, not religious happiness, but only 'belief', which is worthless by comparison. Mediated religion locks the ordinary believer into lifelong dependency: he is like a kidney patient who is chained to his dialysis machine and will never be free of it; he *must* get his regular transfusions of forgiveness and Grace from the ecclesiastical salvation machine. So the prophets and Jesus, like other religious prophets and innovators, want to see the end of the ritual universe and the salvation machine. They look for a new world in which the great distinctions between the divine and the human, the sacred and the profane, the clean and the unclean, and between different degrees of sacred rank have disappeared, so that religion becomes immediate and beliefless: they look for a world without violence and oppression, globalized, post-ethnic, supercommunicative and humanitarian, a world of reciprocally transparent and equal persons, a 'kingdom of ends' in Kant's phrase, and a world in which the divine is no longer objectified but has become scattered and dispersed into people's 'hearts'. They look forward to the sort of world we are now trying to build. Thus the sacred universe, *minus* all the discriminations that built it up, equals the Kingdom of God. Ecclesiastical theology, deconstructed, equals kingdom theology.

We now see two radically different theological interpretations of our present cultural and religious situation opening up before us. For the neo-orthodox, Jesus came to earth 'to found the Church' and to validate the claims of the higher clergy. The developed church and its theology represents a true continuation of his project, and 'Christianity' is most fully itself at the peak of its historical development in the sacred civilization of the high Middle Ages. The secularization of culture that has been accelerating since the Enlightenment represents a rebellion against God, and therefore a movement into nihilism, that was completed by the twentieth century. Postmodernity, acknowledging the failure of secular man's attempt to go it alone, represents the chance to reinstate the old Latin Christian culture. Secular reason is bankrupt, and it is time to return to Augustine.

The radical Christian interpretation of our present situation is entirely different. In our view, Jesus did *not* come to earth 'to found the Church'. He was a prophet of the Kingdom of God, in the hope of which he lived and died. But the Kingdom was delayed, and after his death the Church came into being as a stopgap. It was a disciplinary organization that recruited people and trained them so that they would be ready and waiting for the Kingdom world. But generations went by, and still the Kingdom did not come. The Church gradually changed character: instead of preparing people for the coming of the Kingdom on earth, it now prepared people for divine Judgment and life in the heavenly world after death.[7] It was ruled by the higher clergy who controlled the sacraments, and it began to think of itself as 'indefectible'. It was no longer a merely transitional stage in the religious history of humankind: it was permanent. Ecclesiastical discipline and mediated religion would be the human fate *forever*: it is very noticeable that in ecclesiastical theology religious alienation is sealed in. In the doctrine of Christ and in mystical theology, the God-man disjunction is very strictly maintained. In order to keep undiminished the need for religious mediation, and so for the Church, ecclesiastical theology defers our final salvation and our religious happiness for ever. It is always 'belief', and never enjoyment; for as the White Queen said to Alice, 'the rule is, jam tomorrow and jam yesterday–but never jam today.'

Radical theology cannot endure such severe pessimism. It is committed to deconstructing ecclesiastical theology into kingdom theology, and above all to deconstructing the God-man distinction. It seeks liberation through mysticism,[8] and then through Protestantism. Then it is impelled to attempt to leave the ecclesiastical era behind altogether, and to create the kingdom world on earth. This attempt has taken many forms: congregationalism, Quakerism, 'America', anarchism, socialism, communism, liberal democracy, humanitarian ethics.

Hence our painful and paradoxical present-day condition, as radical theology interprets it. Since the seventeenth century the old Church has forgotten its own merely transitional character, and has lost touch with its own radical tradition of kingdom theology. Instead, the Church has made an absolute of itself, of its own merely mediated kind of religion and its own doctrine system. The Church has declared itself indefectible and inerrant. So it no longer saves, because it no longer knows of anything higher and better than itself. (It is not the True Church any more, because it says that it *is*). Meanwhile the surrounding secular culture of the West has been steadily developing, by the progressive deconstruction and democratization of the old medieval heritage. Led especially by 'America', itself the New World, we still battle against discrimination of every kind: our humanitarian ethics, our feminism, our anti-racism, our political correctness and our environmentalism show us still striving to build the Kingdom of God on earth. The paradoxical result of all this is that today the best secular morality outside the Church represents a much more developed form of Christianity than is available from within the Church. In matters such as the treatment of homosexuals, the Church today needs to learn *its own religion* from what it calls 'the world'.

So for the radical Christian, postmodern culture with its ubiquitous, scattered religiosity and its opposition to discrimination is a secular realization of the traditional Kingdom of God. I don't go quite as far as Mark C. Taylor, who sees in the city of Las Vegas the Kingdom of God on earth,[9] but I do see in our postmodern humanitarian ethics the best realization of the Christian ideal yet seen on earth.

Chapter Nineteen
Practicalities

We are now in a position to draw a number of conclusions about the practicalities of reformation.

Church Christianity originally arose as an interim arrangement that was to fill the period of waiting between Jesus' exaltation to Heaven and his return in glory with the promised Kingdom. The church's job was to gather a substantial — and, as it was decided, international — body of believers and keep them trained, fit and vigilant, so that they would be ready to greet the Lord and to share in his kingdom when it came. The Church was an odd mixture of fifth column, cargo cult and reception committee, and the Apostles were at first its only officers.

The quasi-military and disciplinary role of the Church made it very apt for development into the established religion of a great and multi-ethnic agricultural civilization, and within three or four centuries the Church had indeed become a huge apparatus of mediated religion, like the old Jewish Temple but internationalized. Apostolic authority now justified social authority generally, the Kingdom was postponed until after death, and ordinary believers were now promised that in return for their faith, obedience, and lifelong toil here below they could hope for rest and glory hereafter.

Some paradoxes and dangers arise at this point, for whereas the 'material base' upon which modern society rests is a set of organizational skills (the skills of organizing the acquisition and application of large bodies of knowledge, the techniques of political and economic management, and so forth), in pre-industrial society everyone was highly aware that everything rested only upon the back of the agricultural labourer, Piers Plowman. The cosmic consolation and the promise that the Church offered to Piers Plowman had to be believable – which meant that the Church (that is, the whole symbolic apparatus of mediated religion) needed to be as big and grand and beautiful and convincing as possible. The resulting paradox is that the more thoroughly the Church exploits Piers Plowman in order to make itself great and beautiful at his expense, the more it is *justified* in doing so, because the greater his misery and therefore his need of the consolations of religion.

This paradox created a cul-de-sac. The Church was bound in the end to make a great idol of itself for Piers Plowman's sake, by declaring its dogmas to be certainly and immutably true, and itself indefectible, infallible and altogether necessary for salvation. The Church made itself an absolute, and nobody was to blame, were they? – for the great churchmen were (and still are) perfectly sincere in their pastoral concern for Piers Plowman's spiritual welfare, and Piers Plowman himself genuinely needed and profited from the beauty and the consolations of religion. So long as he remained hemmed in by ignorance, illiteracy and powerlessness, Piers had nowhere else to look to for guidance and comfort except the Church.

But in the early eighteenth century, in the vast Benedictine monasteries of central Europe the Baroque style peaks and goes Rococo – and we see the whole system finally going over the top. It is impossible to be unmoved by the unsurpassed beauties of Steinhausen and Vierzenheiligen, the two loveliest and most hauntingly sad buildings in Europe. After this, one thinks, the Church is doomed. The *conscious illusionism* of the Rococo style reveals that the Church is beginning to know that what it offers to Piers Plowman is all only a magical illusion, a coup de théâtre, a painted veil with nothing whatever behind it. It is all *maya*, a beautiful dream.

From about 1740, I say, the Church itself knows deep in its heart that it no longer really believes its own faith, and every great churchman becomes a Bishop Blougram, someone who in an unbuttoned mood will admit to knowing that he lives in the twilight of faith.[1] In this book I am concluding that for the sake of the future of Christianity we should withdraw our own past over heavy emotional investment in the Church, and our assent to its fatally inflated claims on its own behalf. The Church is stuck up its cul-de-sac, and will not reform itself. Much of the best of the continuing Christian movement has since the mid-eighteenth century continued to develop, but now *outside* the church, in the concern for human emancipation, human rights, humanitarian ethics, liberal democratic politics and so on – so that there is now more that is worth living and dying for outside the church than there is within it.

Distancing ourselves somewhat from the church, we abandon the entire system of supernatural doctrine. There is no supernatural order. There is only this world, our world, the here and now which is the last world we will ever know. We should transfer our Christianity and our desupernaturalized, critical view of the original Jesus and his message wholesale into the 'kingdom' style of religion. We are talking about learning how directly to live the immediate kind of religion. But we are of course not now talking about a *supernatural* realization of the Kingdom of God on earth: we are talking only of a natural or secular realization of the kingdom just by the natural or purely immanent historical development of Christianity. Over the centuries many of the best people have laboured to bring into being the kind of world their religion has taught them to hope for, that's all. Furthermore, as was argued above in relation to the state of Israel,[2] the secular tradition is today much more likely to bring in the world that ancient religion hoped for than is the new aggressive and resentful religious Right.

Today the project of reforming Christianity is the project of working out, learning to live and propagating the 'kingdom' style of religious thinking and living. In many ways, it is church Christianity's other and better half: although it is secular it is nevertheless a perfectly genuine realization of what church Christianity itself still professes to be waiting for, so that it is very convenient to use the church and her language as a 'shell company', or a convenient backdrop against which we can explain kingdom religion and show up what is novel and distinctive about it. I have been using this method for some years. I remain technically a priest in good standing within the church, and although I do not officiate, I do still communicate – the Eucharist being a kingdom rite. I still address a predominantly Christian audience, because this is the milieu in which we have the best chance of making ourselves understood. So I use the church's faith as a backdrop; but I want to avoid getting caught up in the church's traditional dualistic ways of thinking which lead it to overvalue almost everything that belongs to itself and to denigrate almost everything 'worldly' – i.e., independent of itself. The kingdom has left behind the traditional dualism of sacred and secular spheres of life (Church and State, Grace and Nature, City of God and City of Man). Because it is immediate, kingdom religion is impelled to be maximally world affirming and non-dualistic.[3]

To reform Christianity, we must quietly detach ourselves from 'church' ways of thinking and living, and instead develop and propagate the new 'kingdom' ways of thinking and living. This may be done in an anonymous and unlabelled way, as for example by many people in the helping professions and in the great humanitarian aid organizations. A notable contribution is being made by informal religious societies such as Sea of Faith, in which people find out just how closely they are brought together when the basis of their association is not a creed but simply mutual respect for each other's spiritual freedom. There is also a great need for at least some people to explore and expound kingdom religion in writing, as I have been trying to do for some years past: but it is an extraordinarily stressful and difficult task, calling for the abilities of a Kierkegaard. Who today has the strength for it? Kierkegaard when writing his 'second literature', the Christian writings, was in his late thirties, and it killed even *him*: what prospect have we of producing another talent to equal his? In the end, all that need be said about us academics is that we are people who are just about good enough to know who the really good are – and that we are not amongst them. But at least we can all of us learn to practise solar living and, in social ethics, 'humanitarianism in the Void', and we can report the results. *Any* practice of religion without untruth is so novel and wonderful a thing that everyone who seriously attempts it should have something interesting to say about it.

From all this it follows that we do not advocate any personal heroics, or the revolutionary transformation of the church. That would be romantic folly. There will be no new Luther, mainly because the heroic individual genius, the type of individual who was once Europe's special pride, is now historically obsolete. Instead, and in accordance with our generally secular and naturalistic outlook, we should assume that the church will run true to form and opt for slow decline. In which case would-be reformers like me must quietly withdrawn our emotional capital from it, and instead make cool use of it as providing the right contrasting backdrop against which to develop and display the new 'kingdom' type of Christianity.[4]

The problem is gradually, gradually to persuade the church that kingdom religion – immediate religion – really is a fulfilment and not a wickedly reduced version of its faith. Experience teaches that churchpeople invariably regard any updated, rationalized or secularized version of their religion as an odious and mutilated reduction of the holy plenitude of the traditional Faith. For them the painted veil – that is, the whole elaborate symbolic apparatus of mediated religion, every bit of it – just *is* Christianity. For the Orthodox, who are typical, the fulness of Christianity is the fulness of Holy Tradition, a plenum. If you try to show them what is behind the painted veil, what it is that we go into in death, then they will be horrified and outraged. For what is behind the painted veil?

What is it trying to mediate to us? Here are a few answers, all equally good or bad: the divine Abyss; Be-ing; the endlessness, outsidelessness and pure contingency of life; *sunyata* or universal Emptiness; cool Blue. To get its proper meaning and weight, each of these phrases would need to be surrounded by and embedded in a few hundred appropriate words. (Thus, 'Blue' would be explained in terms of the sky in Japan, Dereck Jarman's film *Blue*, Buddhism, nirvana, the Void, and the bliss of passing out into an infinite cool glittering emptiness.) But even as they stand, the phrases are not wrong. They will all do: and of course they will frighten off the ordinary believer who loves the painted veil and wants to cling to it, even and especially in death. The difficult task then is ourselves to live and to write in such a way as to persuade ecclesiastical Christians to throw away their idols and learn the greater happiness of solar living; of saying Yes to the contingency of everything including oneself and all one's own opinions; of saying Yes to Be-ing and the unity of life and death as a single package; of living by 'losing oneself in the objectivity of world love'.[5] Usually, only *writing* can successfully conjure up and communicate the special happiness of the beliefless, immediate, 'kingdom' type of religion. Occasionally we may be very lucky and encounter a person who radiates it. But in general we must be prepared to find that for a very long time yet people will go on saying that kingdom religion is 'not Christianity'. A form of idolatry of the painted veil has been established for a very long time. I am sure that it will not be given up quickly, and it may be that it will never be given up. Hence the semi-detached relationship to the church that I have felt reluctantly compelled to advise. We will have to be cool about this: we will have to let the church go, because we are certainly not going to replace it with anything like it. In the Kingdom there is of course no distinct religious society making exalted claims on its own behalf. It's raison d'être has gone.

Chapter
Twenty

Prospects

I have been stressing the obvious fact that although historic Latin Christianity, both Catholic and Protestant, is currently in steep decline, it has no appetite at all for a new reformation, and is most unlikely to develop one. Its history over a very long period led it to forget its own merely temporary and interim status, and to make exorbitant claims about itself and its doctrines, claims that it cannot now retract. The church's acts and her teachings are divinely guaranteed and protected from error: the church is indefectible and infallible – in fact, the church is the most important institution in all of cosmic history. Her dogmas are certain and immutable truths, and so on, and on. With a self-image like that, it is not exactly surprising that it took the church some 350 years to admit that it ever so slightly mishandled that unfortunate business with Galileo, and it is even less surprising that ever since in the late seventeenth century the Western Churches first began to find themselves forced permanently onto the defensive, no new movement in either religion or theology has been able to attract the church and become firmly entrenched unless it reaffirms orthodoxy. Thus in the Protestant tradition, Pietism, Methodism, Evangelicalism and Pentecostalism were all neo-orthodox. The church is highly protective of tradition, and the internal politics of faith is always tilted towards the established orthodoxy. Critical and liberal theology have failed and failed. At best they have been briefly tolerated, but they have never really been *heard*, and they have never *lasted*.

An extreme example, from the present day, is the imperviousness of the church to biblical scholarship. In spite of two centuries of intensive critical study of the New Testament, preachers all over the West continue to declare every Sunday that "Jesus said 'I am the Way, the Truth and the

133

Life'", without fear of contradiction. They simply disregard the Jesus of history, and go on preaching the muddled and impossible divine Christ of traditional faith and Italian painting. A Chinese wall has been erected between academic theology and the church; and, even more oddly, there is also now a Chinese wall within the little world of academic theology, between the New Testament scholars and the people who teach and write Christian doctrine. The most fashionable of the younger theologians are once again neo-orthodox, and are writing as if their New Testament colleagues in other studies down the same corridor do not exist.

That's very odd, because in recent years the New Testament scholars have produced a large number of good, big and widely read *summae* (full systematic statements) about the historical Jesus.[1] Why is it that all this work has so little effect upon the church, and no effect at all upon the way Christian doctrine is currently being written?

The question is awkward for me: church Christianity is in terminal decline and its divine Christ is (a) a muddle, and (b) never existed. I have for some years tried to argue that fortunately the historical Jesus and his kingdom religion are on the contrary alive and intellectually very interesting. But in a number of ways the evidence is against me. The church and the church's divine Christ *are* indeed fading away – but the historical Jesus is not yet catching on. I have been troubled for years by the thought that he is finally fading out of the consciousness of the West, and perhaps nothing can bring him back. I don't too much mind about losing the church and its version of 'Christianity'; but the loss of Jesus is a far more serious blow.

The trouble is that whereas nobody doubts that ordinary people already have or can soon acquire a reasonably clear and distinct picture of who the Buddha and Muhammad were and what they stood for, Jesus' memory and his legacy seem to have been fatally and permanently blurred and confused by the massive theological transformation of him that began soon after his death.[2] It had already begun to corrupt the surviving traditions about him even before the Synoptic Gospels were written. Modern scholarship might have been able to put that right – but then, the problems were further compounded by the canonization of St John's Gospel, and the church's now irreversible commitment to St John's picture of Jesus as a divine being who has become incarnate in human form in order to reveal his glory to us. When the church locked itself into that view of Jesus, it made itself incapable of ever taking the real Jesus seriously. Finally, the last nail was hammered into the coffin by Albert Schweitzer's (seeming) demonstration that when the message and outlook of the historical Jesus were at last recovered at the end of the nineteenth century, by Johannes Weiss and others, it turned out that he was in any case a figure too strange and remote to be of any use to us.[3] The church could only too easily fall upon Schweitzer's conclusions and read them as justifying its own neglect of the historical Jesus and its perennial theological anti-intellectualism.

The question is not exactly one that is discussed in orthodox doctrinal textbooks, but can we save Jesus? For some years I have adopted the novel strategy of trying to show *indirectly* that Jesus' world view and his teaching are not in fact as alien and impossible to appropriate as has been thought. Hence the talk of 'language's own philosophy', *Philosophy's Own Religion*, and kingdom theology.[4] The idea (well, part of the idea) was to establish philosophically a context in which Jesus could be set and could be heard to be saying something interesting. I can't save Jesus as divine saviour, but I can perhaps do something for him as ethical teacher – provided that you don't mind learning to see him not as a god who can't be wrong, but as a man who might be right. If you will make that concession, then we have a chance of being able to resurrect Jesus, by giving him the philosophical setting in which he can be heard aright. So for the present I make no apology for keeping the name and message of Jesus within my reformed version of Christianity. 'Kingdom religion' can thus be duly credited to its original author, once mummified by theology and now restored to life by philosophy.

If the church is unlikely to warm to any of this, I have some other reasons for hoping that the argument may be going my way and that the long-term prospects are after all quite bright. The argument goes as follows: as the church's claims got higher and her theology became more and more highly elaborated, her world view became more and more dualistic. The process finally peaked in the Catholic and Protestant scholasticism of the seventeenth century, and the resulting splits (for example in the self between body and soul, in life between time and eternity, and in morality between all short-term, earthly and merely instrumental values and the only intrinsic value – namely life's Chief End, the eternal salvation of one's own soul) became acutely painful. The more clearly it was spelled out – as in John Donne's poetry of profane and sacred love – the more it was bound to provoke a sharp reaction. Too sharp a split between body and soul, their respective orientations and claims, is very bad for men and even worse for women. Since the seventeenth century, it is reasonable to see in the rise of the historical consciousness, the rise of the novel, the rise of psychology and especially its adoption of biological ways of interpreting human development, human emotions and behaviour – it is reasonable to see in all this a sustained attempt to heal the old soul/body split and develop a more unified and this-worldly picture of what a human being is. We are trying to get away from the old platonic and ecclesiastical view that in the end the only intrinsic value is the Highest Good, which is eternal and contemplative, and compared with which all this worldly value is merely instrumental. We are trying to bring the old eternal world down into this world, and to become much more short-termist in outlook. Instead of locating life's chief end in the world beyond death, we want to find the highest good in the way we throw ourselves into life in the here and now. Everything that is loved and done and valued must be so just for its own sake, and in the here and now. So whereas for ecclesiastical platonism all value in this life tended to become merely instrumental, for us all value tends to become intrinsic. World and life denial for the sake of eternal salvation is replaced by pure world and life affirmation *now*.

It has been customary to regard this whole process as a secular humanist rebellion against God and a repudiation of Christianity. I have tried to argue that on the contrary we may see in it Christianity's own struggle to advance from its relatively warped ecclesiastical to its final, 'kingdom', stage of development.

The struggle for a more life affirming outlook cannot accurately be pictured as being no more than the fruit of a rebellion against God, for it is taking place, *and is succeeding*, within the church itself. The point can easily be demonstrated by analysing the changes that took place during the latter half of the twentieth century in the officially approved forms for the principal rites of passage. As was remarked in chapter 10 above, the rites have changed considerably. The Roman Catholic priest no longer *exorcises* the baby before baptising it. The Anglican minister no longer explains to the bride and groom that marriage is God's provision for 'such persons as have not the gift of continency', and it is rare nowadays to hear God being thanked at a funeral 'for that it hath pleased thee to deliver this our brother out of the miseries of this sinful world'. The human body is no longer called 'vile' (Latin *vilis*, base, low or cheap).[5]

Thus the movement towards a more this worldly, humanistic and life affirming outlook is manifestly taking place even within the church itself. As it continues, we come more and more to see 'life' as being outsideless, and this world as being the only world and our last world. We try to give up the old, bad habit of looking disapprovingly at the developing secular culture around us, and moaning about its 'materialism', its 'superficiality', its 'selfishness' and so on. Instead we try to learn the new habit of being as consistently affirmative as we can about our life and our world. Gradually, we begin to understand that instead of waiting for eternal life and eternal salvation after death we have got to seize them right now – and we do it by solar living.

All this means that the big Reformation is already taking place. After the Ecclesiastical Reformation, first Protestant and then Catholic, during the sixteenth century, the greater Reformation – that of Christianity *itself* – begins to get under way in the late seventeenth century and has been slowly gathering momentum ever since. It takes place largely outside the church, but its influence is inevitably felt also *within* the church. Thus I am claiming that the larger historical drift, in the long term, is favourable to the reformation of Christianity by its gradual evolution into kingdom religion. We may expect the decay of supernatural doctrine to continue; and that will tend, in the long run, to bring back the historical Jesus and his message.

The crux here is the question of how we deal with our mortality. In the past – in John Donne's time, and perhaps until quite recently – death was seen as waiting at the end of life, and the thought of it very often drove people into the arms of the church. In kingdom religion we do not see death as a fearful event that comes at the end of life. On the contrary:

> Death is not an event in life: we do not live to
> experience death.
> If we take eternity to mean not infinite temporal
> duration but timelessness, then eternal life
> belongs to those who live in the present.
> Our life has no end, in just the way in which our
> visual field has no limits.[6]

In kingdom religion life is endless and outsideless, but we give ourselves to life in the clear-eyed recognition of life's contingency, finitude and transience. Because we do not believe in any metaphysical soul or core self, we give ourselves completely and continuously into life all the time. We are not afraid of death, because we live by dying all the time. We are *passing away* all the time. And our consciousness that we are and have nothing permanent in ourselves, because we are passing away all the time, is our version of Jesus's moral urgency and his eschatological consciousness. Take it all in, assimilate it, and then first mark and then re-read the solar passages of the Sermon on the Mount – and it all makes sense. Surely, he can return.

Postscript

When I wrote my last reformation book, *Radicals and the Future of the Church* (1989), I felt that I ought to risk ending with a sketch of the church of the future — how it will be organized, and what it will actually do. My proposals (on pp.166–173) have been much mocked, so on this present occasion I have kept talk of the practicalities and prospects to the barest minimum. To those who ask for more, I should say that I still rather like the scenario sketched in *Radicals*.

Appendix I:

A Democratic Philosophy of Life

This very short summary of philosophy was written for a Sea of Faith meeting in Newcastle, early in 1998, and subsequently appeared in the Sea of Faith Magazine.

1. Until about two centuries ago human life was seen as being lived on a fixed stage, and as ruled by eternal norms of truth and value. (This old world-picture may nowadays be called "realism", "platonism" or "metaphysics").

2. But now everything is contingent: that is, humanly-postulated, mediated by language and historically-evolving. There is nothing but the flux.

3. There is no Eternal Order of Reason above us that fixes all meanings and truths and values. Language is unanchored.

4. Modern society then no longer has any overarching and authoritative myth. Modern people are "homeless" and feel threatened by nihilism.

5. We no longer have any ready-made or "dogmatic" truth and we have no access to any "certainties" or "absolutes" that exist independently of us.

6. We are, and have to be, democrats and pragmatists who must go along with a current-consensus world-view.

7. Our firmest ground and starting-point is the vocabulary and world-view of ordinary language and everyday life, as expressed for example in such typically modern media as the novel and the newspaper.

8. The special vocabularies and world-views of science and religion should be seen as extensions or supplements built out of the life-world, and checked back against it.

9. Science furthers the purposes of life by differentiating the life-world, developing causal theories, establishing mathematical relationships and inventing technologies.

10. Religion seeks to overcome nihilism, and give value to life. In religion we seek to develop shared meanings, purposes, narratives. Religion's last concern is with eternal happiness in the face of death.

Appendix II:

Kingdom Religion in the Church

I reproduce below part of a letter from a friend who read this book in draft. This friend, who functions happily — and indeed very successfully — within the Church, takes a more optimistic view than I do of the compatibility of kingdom religion with ecclesiastical religion.

As I said on the phone, I agree with you entirely about the contemporary relevance of kingdom religion. For me Jesus' kingdom teaching furnishes a Christian basis for a non-realist, this-worldly religion of transience. I differ with you, though, about the relationship between the Church and the kingdom. In theory they represent opposites: the one concerned with institutional authority, the other with creative spontaneity. But in practice the institution has allowed space for kingdom theology, and kingdom theology has always needed social structures (look at 'Sea of Faith').

I find kingdom-religion more prevalent than you in Jesus's own teaching. Whereas there are 400+ references to 'kingdom' in the Gospels, there are only two to 'church'. There are no creeds in Jesus' teaching, no institutions or rules. I read the Sermon on the Mount, to take your example, as a kingdom manifesto. On the one hand Jesus requires us to live like the lilies and radiate like lamps, but on the other he requires a rigorous self-critical spirit. Jesus recognizes that solar living must also be responsible. But instead of proposing old-style morality to regulate solarity, he suggests a 'negative dialectic' (or even 'deconstructionism'?) based on personal self-criticism and a refusal to judge others. His proposed religion is radically sparse: a personal religious life of charity and prayer which must never be a cause of boasting. As elsewhere, the spirit of Jesus' teaching on religion is to emphasize its dangers.

Was the Church's first dilemma how to continue with Kingdom religion? The temptation to which the Church succumbed was to institutionalize the kingdom by appointing officers (hieros, hierarchy), writing creeds/doctrines, and forming moral rules. Ever since, the institution of the Church has been at odds with its guiding vision of the kingdom. The kingdom is what the Church prays for in the Lord's prayer, but the kingdom means the end of the church. But despite itself, the Church does, here and there, manage to disseminate and promote kingdom religion. I think this is why I am sticking with it. The Church can hardly set itself against all kingdom theology, because the Gospels are full of kingdom theology. I have the perfect rejoinder to my 'churchy' colleagues: to spout scripture back at them!

My best reply to this friend is to point out that ecclesiastical theology is to kingdom-theology as journey to destination, and as means to end. But in practice ecclesiastical theology always makes of itself an end-in-itself. It has all the power: it defines orthodoxy and controls truth. It decides who's in and who's out, and until the power-structure has been overcome kingdom-religion will always be on the defensive, apologizing for itself and begging for toleration.

All of which goes to show that I am still rather dualistic in outlook, seeing things in black and white, and complaining about conflicts that I am myself provoking. Whereas my correspondent, more 'easy, going' than I am, is able to find a modus vivendi without difficulty, and perhaps he exemplifies my own ideas better than I do.

Notes

Preface

1. See Albert Schweitzer, *The Quest of the Historical Jesus*, pp. 478–87. The precise words are cited from *My Life and Thought*, pp. 54–56, quoted by Dennis Nineham in the Foreword to the new edition, p. 24.

2. For the contents of this paragraph, see the evidence marshalled in, for example, Geza Vermes, *The Religion of Jesus the Jew*, chaps. 5 and 6.

Introduction

1. The last attempt at a full-scale Christian metaphysics was arguably Ralph Cudworth's *True Intellectual System of the Universe* (1678), written at a time when it was already clear enough that the Cartesian-mechanistic view of the world was going to prevail, and that Cudworth's own Christian Platonism was in retreat.

2. The main points that need to be made here are well made by Bart D. Ehrman, *The Orthodox Corruption of Scripture*.

Chapter One — **Reforming Christianity**

1. Some of the reasons why this move is now appropriate are given in my *Kingdom Come in Everyday Speech*. The crucial point is this: in the period of the Reformation, the radicals tried to push on from the Church to the Kingdom. Luther (and society as a whole) decided against them, and almost wholly squeezed them out. But their ideas about freedom of thought, conscience, and assembly, their protest against social inequality, and their proto-democratic ideas about Church polity remained. Much of modernity subsequently developed as a secular realization of Christianity's own long-term programme – a fact which the Church has still not fully recognized. Today, Christians *have* to push on to the 'Kingdom' stage in order to catch up with what they call 'the world'.

2. Much of this is of course well said by Dostoyevsky's Grand Inquisitor in the eponymous chapter of *The Brothers Karamazov* (1879–1880). But Dostoyevsky takes the rather easy course of making the Roman Church his chief target, whereas the critique applies to *all* forms of Church Christianity.

Chapter Two — **An Ugly Little Man**

1. See Origen, *Contra Celsum*, VI, 75 (tr. by H. Chadwick, 1953), pp. 388f.
2. Luke 4:23ff.
3. Matthew 27:42.
4. Luke 24:15f., John 20:14, 21:4.

5. See Neil MacGregor with Erika Langmuir, *Seeing Salvation* and *The Image of Christ*. Notice that Neil MacGregor and his associates still take it for granted that the historical Jesus, the Jesus of all four Gospels, and the God Incarnate of fully developed Latin Christianity are all of them one and the same.

6. Notice that my number 17, Christ in the House of Simon the Pharisee, is almost the only non-miraculous scene from Christ's period of public activity that is commonly represented in Christian art.

Chapter Three — Holiness and Leakage

1. See Mary Douglas, *Purity and Danger* and *Natural Symbols*.

2. *Qur'ān* 4, 154-57/155-59; see Geoffrey Parrinder, *Jesus in the Qur'an*, chap. 11.

Chapter Four — The Coming of Immediate Religion

1. *War and Peace*, book 14, chap. 3 in the old Louise and Aylmer Maude translation. The book was translated into French very soon, and was read in French by some of the English Victorians such as Matthew Arnold. But Tolstoy's great impact in Britain comes only with the Maude translations in Edwardian times. Tolstoy's remarkable equation of 'God' with 'life' is as good a definition of any of what 'Immediate Religion' amounts to – namely, a non-realist or 'non-objectifying' view of God.

2. *The New Religion of Life*. The one serious omission from this book that has so far come to light is the remarkable passage from *War and Peace* that has just been quoted.

Chapter Five — Kingdom Religion

1. *Kingdom Come*, pp. 98ff. Compare another summary on pp. 89f.

2. Jeremiah 31:33. The main kingdom theology passages in the Old Testament (or Hebrew Bible) are listed in *Kingdom Come*, pp. 99f.

3. Mark 14:25 (= Matthew 26:29; Luke 22:15–18).

4. From *Kingdom Come*, pp.3f.

5. See my *Philosophy's Own Religion*.

Chapter Six — Outside In

1. Salman Rushdie has one of the characters in *The Ground Beneath her Feet* say that all the world religions are simply wrong: none of them gives anything like a true portrayal of the human situation. And Rushdie has also said the same in his own person; but he is not *quite* accurate, because one needs nowadays to acknowledge that the philosophers of Madhyamika or Middle-Way Buddhism are nearly right. Indeed, they are quite surprisingly nearly right.

2. See my *The New Christian Ethics* (1988). The ideas were new to me at that time, and the book accordingly came out too difficult to be understood.

Chapter Seven — Inside Out

1. Notice that, just as in the old theism God left images of himself, his fingerprints, all over the created world, so nowadays we see images and reflections of ourselves all over our world. But there is a difference: the old Cosmos was relatively stable, and the images of God changed only very slowly, if at all. But nowadays we are part of our world and change rapidly with it, all the time. So the analogies and harmonies between the self and the world are shifting.

Chapter Eight — A Way of Living

1. On all this, see Matthew, chaps. 5–7. Read these chapters with an eye open for the extraordinary contradiction between the passages recommending cautious, secretive, inward church spirituality, and the passages recommending all out, expressive, solar spirituality. Then ask yourself why there has historically been no discussion of this glaring inconsistency.

Chapter Nine — The Problem of Self-Transcendence

1. Open any page of Luther's writings, says Kierkegaard, 'and note in every line the strong pulse beat of personal appropriation' (*Concluding Unscientific Postscript*, p. 327). And Kierkegaard himself sees (religious) truth as 'an objective uncertainty held fast in an appropriation process of the most passionate inwardness' (p. 182). But of course Kierkegaard himself does not quite complete the process of appropriation, turn inside out, and then break through into kingdom religion. He never quite made it, alas.

2. In the thought, principally, of D. F. Strauss, L.A. Feuerbach and Karl Marx.

Chapter Ten — Is Reformation Possible? (1)

1. Amongst Lloyd Geering's recent writings, see especially *Tomorrow's God* and *The World to Come*.

2. A phrase from the Exhortation at the beginning of the rite for the Public Baptism of Infants, in the *Book of Common Prayer* 1662, which is still authorized for use.

3. I write this, having made a recent attempt to read the literature of the 'Alpha' course, written by members of the staff of the (Anglican) Church of Holy Trinity, Brompton in West London.

4. *Why Christianity Must Change or Die*, pp. 220ff.

5. *The New Religion of Life*.

6. Bishop Spong's 'Twelve Theses, and a Call for a New Reformation', first issued May 1998, is conveniently printed in the journal of Robert W. Funk's Westar Institute, *The Fourth R*. For the passage quoted, see p. 4. The issue, titled *The New Reformation*, also contains Robert W. Funk's own 'Twenty-One Theses and

Notes', revised and expanded from the version published in the Appendix to his *Honest to Jesus*.

7. However it should be said that John Robinson, as Suffragan Bishop of Woolwich in 1963 at the time when he published *Honest to God*, was not thrown to the wolves by his Diocesan, Mervyn Stockwood, Bishop of Southwark.

8. See Robert W. Funk, *The Poetics of Biblical Narrative*; and, for the language of Jesus, see the 21st of Funk's 'Theses', p. 9.

9. Funk, *Honest to Jesus*, p.305.

10.'The Four Great Errors', section 8, *Twilight of the Idols*, p. 54.

Chapter Eleven — Is Reformation Possible? (2)

1. There are of course *also* difficulties about the grounds for asserting the distinct personality of the Holy Spirit. To this day, Christian language has never in fact succeeded in ascribing distinct personhood to the Spirit – a clear sign of the dogma's failure.

2. John Hick, *The Myth of God Incarnate*.

3. Senior Churchmen also take flight into history, when instead of saying 'I believe that *p*', they say 'Down the ages the Church has believed that *p*', 'Christians believe that *p*', 'the Bible teaches that *p*', and so on. The device is popular *with audiences*!

4. See chap. 10, n. 1.

5. Mark C. Taylor is the contemporary philosopher of religion with the best insight into the religious significance of contemporary culture.

6. Matthew 22:30, Mark 12:25, Luke 20:34ff.

Chapter Twelve — Framing Reformation

1. Arthur C. Danto, 'The Artworld'. See also B. R. Tilghman, *But is it Art?*

2. A phrase introduced in my *After All*, pp. 8of.

3. D. F. Strauss, *The Christ of Faith*.

Chapter Thirteen —Throwing off the Painted Veil

1. Some years ago a notable Roman Catholic theologian told me that he had suddenly been struck with horror by the thought that the Void begins just the other side of the screen of sense experience.

2. The writer Anthony Burgess, a Roman Catholic, argued in this way at the end of his life: 'It *might* all be true, you know', he would say, apparently in all seriousness, and as if he was thinking that it would be worth calling for a priest when the time came, because one who dies 'fortified by the rites of the Church' stands *either* to gain eternity *or* to lose nothing. Pascal's old and sinister Wager Argument, again.

3. Brian Moore, *No Other Life*. The *leitmotif* phrase that gives the novel its title is first used in chap. 4 by the priest-narrator's dying mother. Her last words are 'There is no other life'. The book describes the career of a brilliant young

black priest, in a Caribbean country halfway between Haiti and Ecuador, who is influenced by Liberation theology and rises to become president of his country.

Chapter Fourteen — **Solarity and History**

1. Mark 3:1–6.
2. Luke 4:16–30.
3. Hitchcock thought of his actors as 'cattle', and in traditional religious thought men were 'the cattle of God' or 'sheep', who needed to be shepherded. Hitchcock was of course a Catholic.
4. Julian Roberts, *German Philosophy*, p. 7.

Chapter Fifteen — **Solar Action**

1. The whole subject remains wildly controversial. Compare Mary Boyce in J. R. Hinnels, *A Handbook of Living Religions*, with the very scornful Julian Baldick in Sutherland's *The World's Religions*.
2. From Mary Boyce in Hinnels, *Handbook*, pp. 178f.
3. For the end of mediated religion, see for example Jeremiah 31:33, and the gospel themes of the destruction of the Temple and the rending of the Temple veil. For the distribution of the divine Spirit, see Joel 2:28f.
4. When the End comes, long-term planning and instrumental thinking are exposed as absurd, e.g. Luke 12:16–20. Nothing can be concealed any longer; everything is floodlit, e.g. Luke 11:33–36. People live entirely in the present, Matt 6:25–34.
5. The external Law (which people did not keep) is to be replaced by a law written on the heart. St Paul takes up the theme, in 2 Corinthians 3, and is eloquently humanitarian in his ethics of sympathy.
6. Pentecost reverses Babel, and nationalism is transcended in the new world. In the prophet Isaiah, for example, the new age comes not just to vindicate Israel, but is for the sake of all peoples, e.g. 25:6–9. In early Christian art and writing Christ is enthroned upon the cosmos, symbolizing the final complete appropriation of the physical world by the human world.
7. Acts 2:41–47, 4:32–37, etc.
8. See my *The New Religion of Life*.
9. D. H. Lawrence, 'The Man's World', chap. 23 in *The Rainbow*.
10. See Don Cupitt, *Solar Ethics*, p. 2.

Chapter Sixteen — **One World**

1. This rather simple way of making the radical humanist point – everything is channelled through us, because it is we and only we in whom the world becomes conscious of itself *as* world, bright, finished, known – is often pointed out by otherwise unphilosophical scientists. I tried to develop it a little philosophically in the two Being books of 1998: *The Religion of Being* and *The Revelation of Being*.

2. Joshua 24:15; 2 Corinthians 6:2 (RSV).

Chapter Seventeen — The Dream of a Perfect Society

1. On this theme see my *Kingdom Come*. Religion is currently more potent and interesting in its dispersed and scattered-everywhere form than in its ecclesiastically concentrated form,.

2. E.g., Zechariah 8:22.f.

Chapter Eighteen — Nihilism and Humanitarianism

1. Malachi 1:2–3.

2. On the relation of the early Derrida to the *Genesis* creation myth, see Eve Tavor Bannett, *Structuralism*, chap. 4.

3. See my *Kingdom Come*, Appendix Two, 'Inequalities'.

4. Reproduced in John R. Hinnells (ed.), *A Handbook of Living Religions*, pp. 76f.

5. John Milbank, *Theology and Social Theory*, etc.

6. On humanitarianism, see for example *Kingdom Come*, chap. 7; and my 'Humanitarian Ethics' in the forthcoming Hebblethwaite *Festschrift*, ed. Julius Lipner. For the connection between humanitarianism and nihilism, the best starting point is still Albert Camus's novel *La Peste* (1947), E.T. *The Plague* (1948).

7. On the deferral of the Kingdom and its consequences, see the fine late essay by Albert Schweitzer, 'The Conception of the Kingdom of God in the Transformation of Eschatology . . . '.

8. See my *Mysticism After Modernity*, which is about the consequences of the fact that the Church only promises salvation, and cannot actually deliver it.

9. Mark C. Taylor, *About Religion,* chap. 7: 'The Virtual Kingdom'; and *The Réal: Las Vegas NV* (CD-ROM, issued in the US with the book).

Chapter Nineteen — Practicalities

1. See Robert Browning's poem 'Bishop Blougram's Apology'.

2. Chap. 17, above, pp.133f.

3. This was a key theme of *The New Christian Ethics*. I was attempting to describe a purely affirmative and non-dualistic moral outlook.

4. Compare this account of our present and future relation to the Church with the one I gave in *Radicals and the Future of the Church*. The Church's situation and religious prospect have deteriorated significantly in only a decade or so.

5. A phrase from my *Solar Ethics*, p. 56.

Chapter Twenty — Prospects

1. For example, Gerd Theissen and Annette Merz, *The Historical Jesus;* Gerd Lüdemann, *Jesus after Two Thousand Years;* many well-known works by E.P. Sanders and Geza Vermes; and in the US, the works of several writers associated

with R.W. Funk and the Jesus Seminar. The latter group have tried harder than anyone else to encourage the laity to question the way Jesus is presented to them in Church.

2. Bart D. Ehrman, *The Orthodox Corruption of Scripture*, reminds one of how little scruple, compared with us, ancient writers had about this.

3. I refer here to the impression given to the English-speaking world by the standard translation of the first edition of *The Quest of the Historical Jesus*. That impression needs to be corrected, now that the full text of the much revised and enlarged second edition of 1913 is available in English (London: SCM Press 2000).

4. E.g. Don Cupitt, *The Meaning of It All*, pp.104ff.; *Kingdom Come*; and *Philosophy's Own Religion*.

5. The phrases quoted in this paragraph are all taken from the English *Book of Common Prayer* 1662, which remains authorized for use, but is in practice now superseded.

6. Ludwig Wittgenstein, *Tractatus Logico-Philosophicus*, 6.4311. I have added a comma in the third sentence. And, come to think of it, Wittgenstein was very 'kingdom'.

Bibliography

Bannett, Eve Tavor. *Structuralism and the Logic of Dissent: Barthes, Derrida, Foucault, Lacan.* London and New York: Macmillan. 1989.

Cupitt, Don. *After All: Religion without Alienation.* London: SCM Press, 1994.

Cupitt, Don. *Kingdom Come in Everyday Speech.* London: SCM Press, 2000.

Cupitt, Don. *The Meaning of It All in Everyday Speech.* London: SCM Press, 1999.

Cupitt, Don. *Mysticism After Modernity*, Oxford: Blackwell, 1988.

Cupitt, Don. *The New Christian Ethics.* London: SCM Press, 1988

Cupitt, Don. *The New Religion of Life in Everyday Speech*, London: SCM Press, 1999.

Cupitt, Don. *Philosophy's Own Religion.* London: SCM Press, 2000.

Cupitt, Don. *Radicals and the Future of the Church.* London: SCM Press, 1989

Cupitt, Don. *The Religion of Being.* London: SCM Press, 1998.

Cupitt, Don. *The Revelation of Being.* London: SCM Press, 1998.

Cupitt, Don. *Solar Ethics.* London: SCM Press, 1995.

Danto, Arthur C. 'The Artworld'. *Journal of Philosophy* 61 (1964), pp.571–84.

Douglas, Mary. *Natural Symbols: Explorations in Cosmology.* London: Barrie and Rockliff, 1970; Pelican Books 1973.

Douglas, Mary. *Purity and Danger: An Analysis of the Concepts of Pollution and Taboo* 1966, London: Routledge and Kegan Paul, 1984.

Ehrman, Bart D. *The Orthodox Corruption of Scripture: The Effect of Early Christological Controversies on the Text of the New Testament.* New York: Oxford University Press, 1993.

Funk, Robert W. *Honest to Jesus: Jesus for a New Millennium.* HarperSanFrancisco, 1996.

Funk, Robert W. *The Poetics of Biblical Narrative.* Sonoma, CA: Polebridge Press, 1988.

Funk, Robert W. 'Twenty-One Theses and Notes'. *The Fourth R* 11,4 (July–August 1998), pp. 8–10.

Geering, Lloyd. *Tomorrow's God: How we Create our Worlds.* Wellington, NZ: Bridget Williams, 1994; reprint Santa Rosa, CA: Polebridge Press, 2000.

Geering, Lloyd. *The World to Come: From Christian Past to Global Future.* Santa Rosa CA: Polebridge Press, 1999.

Hick, John (ed.). *The Myth of God Incarnate.* London: SCM Press, 1977.

Hinnels, John R. (ed.). *A Handbook of Living Religions.* Pelican Books, 1985.

The Image of Christ: The catalogue of the exhibition Seeing Salvation (National Gallery, London). Yale University Press, 2000.

Lüdemann, Gerd. *Jesus after Two Thousand Years.* London: SCM Press, 2000.

Kierkegaard, *Concluding Unscientific Postscript*. Swenson-Lowrie translation. Princeton University Press,1941.

MacGregor, Neil, with Erika Langmuir. *Seeing Salvation: Images of Christ in Art*, London: BBC, 2000.

Milbank, John. *Theology and Social Theory: Beyond Secular Reason*. Oxford: Blackwell, 1990.

Moore, Brian. *No Other Life*. London: Bloomsbury Publishing, 1993.

Nietzsche, Friedrich. *Twilight of the Idols* (= *Götzen-Dämmerung*, 1889). Trans. R. J. Hollingdale. Penguin Classics, 1968.

Origen, *Contra Celsum*. Trans. and with an Introduction by H. Chadwick. Cambridge University Press, 1953.

Parrinder, Geoffrey. *Jesus in the Qur'an*. Oxford: Oneworld, 1995.

Roberts, Julian. *German Philosophy*. Cambridge: Polity Press, 1988.

Robinson, J. A. T. *Honest to God*. London: SCM Press, 1963.

Schweitzer, Albert. 'The Conception of the Kingdom of God in the Transformation of Eschatology . . . '. Reprinted in E. N. Mozley's *The Theology of Albert Schweitzer* (1950), and Walter Kaufmann (ed.), *Religion from Tolstoy to Camus*. New York: Harper Torchbooks, 1964.

Schweitzer, Albert. *My Life and Thought*. Eng. trans. 1933. London: A. and C. Black, 1933.

Schweitzer, Albert. *The Quest of the Historical Jesus*. First complete edition. Ed. John Bowden. SCM Press, 2000.

Spong, John Shelby. 'Twelve Theses, and a Call for a New Reformation'. *The Fourth R* 11,4 (July–August 1998), pp. 4–6.

Spong, John Shelby. *Why Christianity Must Change or Die*. HarperSanFrancisco, 1998.

Strauss, D. F. *The Christ of Faith and the Jesus of History: A Critique of Schleiermacher's 'Life of Jesus'*. 1865

Sutherland, Stewart, and others. *The World's Religions*. London: Routledge, 1988.

Taylor, Mark C. *About Religion: Economies of Faith in Virtual Culture*, Chicago: Chicago University Press, 1999.

Theissen, Gerd, and Annette Merz. *The Historical Jesus*, London: SCM Press, 1998.

Tilghman, B.R. *But is it Art?: The Value of Art and the Temptation of Theory*. Oxford: Basil Blackwell, 1984.

Wittgenstein, Ludwig. *Tractatus Logico-Philosophicus*. Trans. by D. F. Pears and B. F. McGuinness. London: Routledge, 1961.

Vermes, Geza. *The Religion of Jesus the Jew*. London: SCM Press, 1993.

Index of Scripture

Index of Names & Subjects